HAUNTED AMERICA

Publications International, Ltd.

Written by J.K. Kelley and James Willis

Photography from Shutterstock.com

Louis Weber, CEO
Publications International, Ltd.
8140 Lehigh Avenue
Morton Grove, IL 60053

ISBN: 978-1-68022-843-4

Manufactured in Canada.

8 7 6 5 4 3 2 1

TABLE OF CONTENTS

INTRODUCTION

Not all hauntings are sinister and not all are as friendly as the caricatured Casper, but most—no matter the situation—are able to bring on a severe case of the howling fantods. You may know there's an eldritch presence in your house, but what are you going to do about it? Move out? Address the enigma to try to agree on a peaceful living arrangement? Try to turn a blind eye and ignore the signs?

Most places across the nation have a complex history that has been swept under the rug by the broom of time, but not everything wants to be forgotten. People identify with where they're from, their family and heritage, their passions and professions, and they may have a hard time letting that identity go once they've given up the ghost. They're left in the liminal space of being an ethereal being in a material world, leaving those of us who do not quite understand the state they're in with an onminous and unsettled feeling in the bottom of our stomachs.

Whether ghosts are the vestiges of our ancestors spectrally guarding us, or something more sinister looking to take advantage of our physical being, they undoubtedly inhabit the spaces around us. The history of America still lives. Historic battlefields are still marched on by regiments from the Other Side. Beautiful mansions still house the ancestral heads of the estate. Suburbs and communities tremble under the pressure of their troubled pasts. *Haunted America* roams across the nation to highlight the best of these paranormal hotspots that are scattered from coast to coast. Get to know the signs and be sure to inform yourself of the taboo history that no one wants to talk about.

CHAPTER 1

PARANORMAL 101

EVERYTHING YOU ALWAYS WANTED TO KNOW ABOUT GHOSTS

When it comes to the paranormal, there are believers and nonbelievers, but no matter where you stand, you have to admit that the thought of an afterlife is intriguing. But how much do you really know about the spirit world?

SO WHAT IS A GHOST, ANYWAY?

A ghost is simply the spirit of a person who has died but has not yet made it to the "Other Side." In other words, it's caught between this world and the next. Ghosts are made up of energy and exist on this plane without a corporeal body. They are often the spirits of people who died suddenly as a result of murder, suicide, or tragic accidents and, thus, were not prepared for death. Sometimes ghosts appear to warn or guide family members, or to share in times of joy, such as the birth of a child.

WHY CAN CHILDREN SEE GHOSTS MORE EASILY THAN ADULTS?

Children are more sensitive to seeing spirits for several reasons. First, they are generally more open-minded and willing to accept things that are new and different. Also, studies have shown that kids are better able to see wavelengths in the lower-light spectrum than adults. Spiritually, children are more closely connected to their heavenly origins than adults. And adults may not be as willing to admit that they saw a ghost for fear of being ridiculed.

CAN GHOSTS CROSS WATER?

The relationship between ghosts and water is the subject of great debate, but the short answer is yes. In fact, most experts agree that ghosts are actually *attracted* to water. After all, spirits are made up of energy, and there's no better conductor of energy than water. That's why you'll often see a great deal of paranormal activity on and near bodies of water.

CAN GHOSTS REALLY FLOAT ABOVE THE GROUND?

Yep. Ghosts are made up of energy, and from what we understand, the spirit world works a bit like electricity. Specters appear to float because when they touch the ground, they are absorbed by the earth—or, electrically speaking, "grounded." That doesn't mean that all ghosts float through the air: Some apparitions seem to be walking without their feet touching the ground. The sound of ghostly footsteps? Well, that's a different mystery entirely.

CAN GHOSTS ATTACH THEMSELVES TO PEOPLE?

Definitely. When spirits remain earthbound, it is often because they have unfinished business. They are usually drawn to specific locations—such as places where they lived, worked, or died—or to people who conjure up strong emotions—either good or bad. Occasionally, a ghost will attach itself to a stranger because that person is able to see or hear it, but that relationship generally only lasts until the spirit's earthly issues are resolved and it crosses over.

HOW DO GHOSTS MOVE OBJECTS OR MANIPULATE ELECTRICAL DEVICES?

Ghosts use energy—both their own essence and borrowed power—to move objects, make noises, play tricks, and get people's attention. Because spirits are made up of energy, they can gather additional fuel from electronic and battery-powered objects. It takes a lot of energy for spirits to communicate, so they need to "charge their batteries" in order to make their presence known. That's why a person living in or visiting a haunted location will sometimes notice that fully charged batteries are drained and other electronic equipment malfunctions. By the same token, ghosts can use their energy to control other technology.

WHERE IS THE BEST PLACE TO SEE A GHOST?

Ghosts can be found just about anywhere, but some of the places where they are most commonly seen are cemeteries, old houses, battlefields, hospitals, colleges and restaurants.

ARE THERE DIFFERENT TYPES OF GHOSTS?

RESIDUAL HAUNTINGS

One type of ghost is known as a residual, which gets its name from the term *residue,* or the idea that something was left behind. Simply put, a residual ghost is believed to be nothing more than energy that is left behind when someone dies. A residual spirit is often explained using the metaphor of an old movie projector that, over time, stores up enough energy that it switches on, plays a short scene, and then shuts back off. For that reason, residuals can be identified by the fact that they always perform the same actions over and over again, never varying what they do. They do not interact with the living.

A residual ghost is believed to be the result of an activity that an individual executed frequently while he or she was alive or the result of a violent, unexpected death—which may explain why so many battlefields are supposedly haunted. In both cases, the release of energy leaves an imprint on the area. A violent death typically results in a sudden release of energy, while a repeated activity results in smaller, more sustained releases. In both cases, it is believed that the released energy is stored in a specific location and somehow replays itself from time to time. For example, the routine of a man who for 50 years would walk from the dining room onto the porch and smoke a pipe every night after dinner might end up causing enough residual energy to linger after the man passes that the action continues to repeat itself. Similarly, a phantom scream that is consistently heard at the same time of day or night could be the result of a residual spirit reenacting its violent death and its last moments among the living.

INTELLIGENT GHOSTS

Unlike residuals, intelligent ghosts not only interact with the living, they tend to seek them out—hence the term *intelligent*. And whereas a residual haunting repeats the same action in the same place, intelligent ghosts are free to roam wherever they please. So if you sometimes see a particular ghost late at night in the kitchen and at other times in the attic in broad daylight, you are dealing with an intelligent. These are believed to be the spirits of people who, for whatever reason, simply refused to move on after they passed away. In some cases, it's because they want to remain with the people and places they loved while they were alive; other intelligents seem to have unfinished business on this plane. And since intelligents seem to be aware of the living, they are the ghosts that most often make themselves known to us and to mediums. Unlike residuals, intelligents seem to have the ability to communicate from beyond the grave.

THE BLACK SHEEP OF THE INTELLIGENT FAMILY

Two rather intriguing subcategories of intelligents are demonic entities and poltergeists. Exactly who or what demonic entities are varies depending on your religious beliefs, but they are still defined as intelligents because they appear to understand that the living are nearby. In other words, demonic entities have been known to interact with humans, which means that they are intelligents. The same would be true for nonhuman ghosts, such as those of dogs, cats, and other animals. If spirits acknowledge or interact with the living, they are intelligents.

The categorization of poltergeists is a topic that is hotly debated. Some believe that because humans appear to be the targets of poltergeist activity—such as flying plates and glasses—they are intelligents. But others believe that the flying objects are caused by nothing more than violent releases of energy, which would make poltergeists residual. Finally, some even believe that poltergeist activity is the result of irregular brain waves from the living, which would make them non-ghostly. So for now, the jury is still out on poltergeists.

GEARING UP FOR GHOSTS

So you've decided you want to go ghost-hunting. Here's a handy list of essential tools every good ghost hunter should have during an investigation.

Electromagnetic Field (EMF) Detector: Generally speaking, a ghost is nothing more than a form of energy. Therefore, it is believed that such energy can be measured as it interacts with other forms of energy, such as those with an electric or a magnetic charge. An EMF detector allows ghost hunters to measure and track anything with these types of charges in a specific area. Look for strange spikes that could be paranormal in nature. EMF detectors, which range in cost from $20 to $75, come in a variety of shapes and sizes, and some even come with LED screens.

Digital Voice Recorder: If you're interested in capturing the voices of the dead, known as electronic voice phenomena (EVP), you'll want to bring along a digital voice recorder. These devices allow you to record voices and otherworldly sounds that the unaided human ear can't detect.

Still Camera: They say a picture is worth a thousand words, so make sure you have a camera at the ready if and when a ghost decides to make an appearance. Any camera will do, but digital cameras are more appealing because the results can be viewed immediately.

Video Camera: If your budget allows (or if you can borrow one), a video camera can serve multiple purposes during an investigation. Not only can you possibly capture paranormal activity, but the built-in microphone can also help pick up ghostly voices and sounds.

Thermometer: Some people believe that a ghost can draw heat energy out of the air, which results in the infamous "cold spot." Therefore, many ghost hunters bring along thermometers to track sudden drops in temperature that might be otherworldly in nature. There are two main types of thermometers: noncontact "spot" thermometers, which measure the temperature of a specific solid object, and ambient thermometers, which measure the temperature of a general area.

Household Items: There are a few household items you might want to bring along on an investigation:

Watch: to note the time of any ghostly activity

Notebook: to record the time and location of above-mentioned activity

Flashlight: to avoid having to walk into dark, haunted rooms

GOING ON A GHOST HUNT

So you're getting ready to go on your very first ghost hunt. How exciting! But what exactly are you getting yourself into? And what's going to happen? Will you encounter shadowy shapes moving around you, hear phantom footsteps, or even see a full-bodied apparition? Read on to find out what to expect—straight from our experts.

"DO I NEED TO DO ANYTHING TO PREPARE FOR THE HUNT?"

Try not to overexert yourself on the day of the investigation, and try to sleep well the night before. Don't eat a huge meal right before the hunt, as that may make you sleepy. Be sure to bring along some water and snacks; being tired, hungry, or dehydrated can impact your senses, possibly making you see, feel, or hear things that don't really exist. Your mood could also impact the investigation.

"WHAT'S THE FIRST THING I SHOULD DO WHEN I GET THERE?"

Familiarize yourself with your surroundings. I like to spend a few minutes sitting quietly and absorbing as many of the sights, sounds, and even smells of the location as possible. As the night progresses, you'll find this extremely helpful in determining whether or not the phenomena you're experiencing are of a paranormal nature.

Also, because you'll probably be spending a lot of time in the dark, it helps to know your way around the location. That way, you won't be so concerned with groping your way through the darkness that you inadvertently miss any paranormal activity around you.

"WHAT SORT OF THINGS WILL I DO DURING A GHOST HUNT?"

Unlike ghost hunts on television shows, which condense entire investigations into 30- or 60-minute segments, a full ghost hunt lasts several hours. Be prepared to spend a lot of time sitting around in the dark waiting for something to happen.

Some paranormal investigation groups like to separate the participants into smaller groups and assign them to specific areas of the haunted site. After about an hour, the groups rotate so that everyone gets ample time in each area.

While at a location, you may be asked to take photos and note any temperature changes or spikes in electromagnetic field readings, which may indicate paranormal activity.

You might also take part in EVP (electronic voice phenomenon) sessions, during which you can ask any spirits present questions in the hope of recording otherworldly responses.

Even if you don't have access to some of the sophisticated ghost-hunting gear that's on the market these days, you can always rely on your senses to "feel" the room and see if you notice anything out of the ordinary.

"WHAT CAN I EXPECT TO SEE?"

If you're lucky, you just might see a ghost! But once again, it's important to get used to your surroundings. You're most likely going to be spending a lot of time in the dark, so make sure that your eyes adjust to the lack of light. "Shadow people"—moving shadows that are seen out of the corner of one's eye—are among the most commonly spotted paranormal phenomena. Should you see a shadow person, take a look around to make sure that what you saw was not caused by something playing tricks on your eyes. For example, nearby streetlights can often cause tree branches blowing in the wind to cast odd shadows.

If you get really lucky, you might see what many consider the "Holy Grail" of the ghost-hunting world: a full-bodied apparition. Should this happen, try to remain calm and observe as much as possible, such as the specter's attire, its actions, and whether or not it seems to know that you're there. This information might help you to determine who the ghost was in life and, more importantly, why it's still hanging around.

"WILL I HEAR GHOSTS TALKING AND ALL SORTS OF WEIRD NOISES?"

Yes, you'll probably hear lots of weird noises. Every site has its own unique set of normal noises (houses settling, animals wandering through, etc.), but because the location is new to you, everything is going to sound a bit spooky. It will be up to you to decide which noises are normal and which might be *para*normal in nature. Typically, when I hear a strange noise during an investigation, I call out, "If that was you, could you please make that noise again?" If the noise repeats, it will help you figure out where it came from, which will, in turn, allow you to determine if there is a natural explanation for it.

Of course, you are likely to hear voices at some point in the evening. Even if all of your fellow ghost hunters are accounted for, consider that sounds can carry quite far, especially if you're in an empty building. If you hear a "disembodied voice," make note of how it sounded and what it said; perhaps ask it to repeat itself or talk louder.

"WHAT WILL I LEARN?"

First and foremost, you'll learn that ghost-hunting TV shows tend to overdramatize situations. You probably won't encounter any ghosts that pick you up and toss you around the room; instead, you'll likely spend most of the investigation sitting quietly in the dark, waiting for something to happen. And if and when something *does* happen, the event will be so fleeting that you might not even notice it until you review your video and audio recordings from the hunt.

But above all, you will learn that ghost hunts are truly unique opportunities to explore the Other Side in an attempt to unravel the age-old mystery of what happens to us after we die. Have fun!

CAN GHOSTS HURT PEOPLE?

One of the most frequent questions that ghost hunters are asked is: "Can ghosts hurt people?" Now that's an intriguing question! We can answer it by observing stories about ghosts.

To answer this question, we have to consider the different kinds of ghosts. Some are no more than shadows or voices, and others are just blips of energy that cause the needle on an EMF detector to twitch. Then there are the translucent apparitions that float down hallways and the forms that are so lifelike that you'd never know that they're ghosts if they didn't vanish before your very eyes. Some spirits, which are known as "intelligents," are thought to be able to communicate with the living. Others, which are known as "residuals," are thought to be far more common and are simply forms of energy reenacting scenes from their life.

Each type of ghost has different abilities. Some are capable of throwing objects across a room, or pressing down on a person's chest while he or she is in bed, or, in rare cases, even possessing people. So if some entities can throw things, it's fair to assume that they can throw things *at* the living.

However, there's some good news behind all of this: If ghosts can hurt people, they very rarely do. Some cases, such as that of the Bell Witch, indicate that ghosts have killed people, but such cases are so rare that we're still talking about the Bell Witch haunting nearly two centuries later.

But there's also one slightly frightening thing to consider: Ghosts don't actually have to exist in order to hurt people. A person can be shocked into falling down stairs or even into having a heart attack, merely by *thinking* that he or she has seen a ghost! And being in an allegedly haunted place can certainly play tricks on your mind. It's never safe to let your imagination run wild when you're tromping around a creepy, dark basement.

So don't be concerned about being whisked away to the Other Side by a woman in white, and if you do encounter flatware flying across the room, duck! Chances are, it won't fly directly *at* you, but you can still get hurt if you don't keep your wits about you.

5 WAYS TO GET RID OF A GHOST

Something strange in your neighborhood? Something weird and it don't look good? Here's a do-it-yourself guide to ghost-busting. But please note: in the world of ghost-busting, there are no guarantees, so proceed at your own risk.

1. **Give it a good talking-to:** The first tactic is simply to ask your ghost, politely but firmly, to leave. If you think the ghost is hanging around the physical world because of fear of punishment in the spirit world, tell it that it will be treated with love and forgiveness. Try not to show anger (which may give a negative spirit more power) or fear (since it's unlikely that a spirit will be able to harm you, especially in your own home).

2. **Clean and serene:** If tough talking doesn't work, the next step is a spiritual cleansing or "smudging." Open a window in each room of your home, then light a bundle of dry sage and walk around with it (have something handy to catch the ashes), allowing the smoke to circulate while you intone the words: "This sage is cleansing out all negative energies and spirits. All negative energies and spirits must leave now through the windows and not return." Do this until you sense that the negative energy has left the building (and before you set fire to the house), and then say, "In the name of God, this room is now cleansed."

3. **Bless this house:** If smudging doesn't do the trick, it may be time to call in the professionals. Ask a local priest or minister to come to your home and bless it. There is usually no charge for this service, but you might be expected to make a small donation to the church.

4. **The Exorcist:** Exorcism is usually carried out by clergy using prayers and religious items to invoke a supernatural power that will cast out the spirit. Roman Catholic exorcism involves a priest reciting prayers and invocations, often in Latin. The priest displays a crucifix

and sprinkles holy water over the place, person, or object believed to be possessed. Exorcism has been sensationally depicted in movies but it's no laughing matter—in the past, people who would now be diagnosed as physically or mentally ill have undergone exorcism, sometimes dying in the process.

5. **What not to do:** Don't be tempted to use Ouija boards, tarot cards, or séances, as these may "open the door" to let in other unwanted spirits. Also be very suspicious of anyone offering a commercial ghost-busting service, including any medium or spiritual adviser who offers to rid your home of a spirit in return for payment. They're almost certain to be charlatans, and you're unlikely to get your money back if their services don't work.

CHAPTER 2

THE NORTHEAST

WEST POINT'S SPIRITED RESIDENTS

The United States Military Academy at West Point has an illustrious history. Since 1802, it has educated young men (and women, beginning in 1976) preparing to serve their country as officers in the U.S. Army; prior to that time, West Point was a military fort. With that much history, it's no surprise that these hallowed halls are home to a ghost or two.

MISS MOLLY

Keeping in line with the pomp and circumstance of the academy, cadets and visitors have reported seeing soldiers from different eras in full-dress uniforms. And back in the 1920s, a spirit inhabiting a house on Professor's Row had to be exorcised. It is unknown whether this was a malevolent ghost or a demonic force, but whatever it was and whatever it did, it frightened two servant girls so terribly that they ran out of the house screaming in the middle of the night.

A cranky Irish cook named Molly is thought to haunt the superintendent's mansion, where she once worked. "Miss Molly"—as she was called when she lived there in the early 19th century—was the maid of Brigadier General

Sylvanus Thayer. A hard worker even in death, Molly is often seen kneading bread in the mansion's kitchen.

THE PICKPOCKET POLTERGEIST

In October 1972, demonologists Ed and Lorraine Warren were invited to give a lecture at West Point. While they were there, they were asked to investigate some paranormal activity that had been occurring at the superintendent's house. It seems that, among other things, personal items and wallets of guests had come up missing...only to be discovered later, neatly arranged on the dresser in the master bedroom.

Lorraine was able to communicate with the "Pickpocket Poltergeist," who identified himself as a man named Greer. In the early 1800s, he had been wrongly accused of murder, and although he was ultimately exonerated, he was anguishing in sorrow and was unable to move on. Lorraine urged him to go into the light.

ROOM 4714

It is Room 4714 in the 47th Division Barracks that has caused the most supernatural speculation. Paranormal activity was first reported there shortly after the Warrens' visit, when students Art Victor and James O'Connor shared the room. One day, when O'Connor went to take a shower, he noticed that his bathrobe was swinging back and forth—but nothing was blowing it. Then suddenly, the temperature in the room dropped several degrees.

A couple of days later, O'Connor saw an apparition of a soldier wearing a uniform and carrying a musket. The following evening, both boys felt an extreme drop in temperature and then saw a man's upper body float through the room; it hovered between the floor and ceiling for a few minutes before disappearing.

One night shortly thereafter, two fellow cadets— Keith Bakken and Terry Meehan—volunteered to spend the night in Room 4714. During the night, Meehan awoke and caught a glimpse of a ghostly figure near the ceiling. By the time Bakken woke up, the apparition was gone, but both boys experienced an extreme drop in temperature. After the campus newspaper published an article about the strange activity, several other cadets offered to sleep in the room. A thermocouple was used to scientifically measure any temperature changes. The coldest temperature was always found right next to O'Connor. Oddly, one night when other cadets were in his room waiting for the ghost, O'Connor saw the specter in *another* room while the boys in Room 4714 saw nothing.

Although a significant number of cadets saw the apparition and felt the drastic temperature change in Room 4714, the identity of this spirit remains unknown. The 47th Division barracks are located near the site of a disastrous house fire that killed an officer. The building is also close to a graveyard in which some Revolutionary War era soldiers are buried. Could the ghost be one of these military men attempting to bond with the new breed of cadet? If so, the spirit eventually gave up—it hasn't been seen or felt since the 1970s.

POPPING HIS TOP: THE SEAFORD POLTERGEIST

Poltergeists are the publicity hounds of the spirit world. While other ghosts are content to appear in the shadows and then vanish so that nobody's ever exactly sure what they saw, poltergeist activities are always very flashy and conspicuous. Need furniture rearranged or doors opened or slammed shut? How about knickknacks moved around or plates smashed? If so, just call your neighborhood poltergeist; they love to perform such mischief in plain sight. Poltergeists don't care—they aren't part of the ghostly union. They just enjoy annoying (and scaring) the living.

POP! POP! POP!

The science of investigating poltergeist activity has come a long way since the days when people blamed it all on witchcraft. One of the cases that got folks thinking that there might be more to it was the story of the Seaford Poltergeist.

This entity first made itself known to the Herrmann family of Seaford, Long Island, in early February 1958. Mrs. Herrmann had just welcomed her children Lucille and Jimmy home from school when several bottles in various rooms of the house all popped their tops and spewed their contents all over. The family considered various explanations, such as excess humidity or pressure building up in the bottles, but the tops were all of the twist-off variety. Short of a miniature tornado yanking the tops off, there seemed to be no rational explanation.

After the same thing happened several more times, Mr. Herrmann began to suspect that his son Jimmy—who had an interest in science—was somehow pulling a fast one on the family. However, after carefully watching the child while the incident happened, Herrmann knew that unless his son was a future Einstein, there was no way that the boy could be responsible. With no "ghost busters" to consult, Mr. Herrmann did the next best thing he could in 1958: He called the police.

Dubious at first, the police launched an investigation after witnessing some of the episodes firsthand. But answers were not forthcoming, and the incidents kept occurring. Even having a priest bless the house and sprinkle holy water in each of its rooms didn't help. An exorcism was considered but rejected because the incidents didn't resemble the work of a demon. Rather, they seemed to be the antics of a poltergeist (a noisy spirit).

EXPLANATION UNKNOWN

Word of the events attracted the attention of the media as well as curiosity seekers. All explanations—from the scientifically sound (sonic booms, strong drafts, freakish magnetic waves) to the weird and wacky (Soviet satellite *Sputnik*)—were considered and dismissed. Although this was the Cold War era, it was unclear how tormenting a single American family fit into the Soviets' dastardly scheme of world domination. What was far more worrisome was that the incidents seemed to be escalating in violence. Instead of just bottles popping open, objects such as a sugar bowl, a record player, and a heavy bookcase were tossed around. Fortunately, help soon arrived in the form of experts from Duke University's Parapsychology Laboratory. Their theory was that someone in the house was unwittingly moving objects via Recurrent Spontaneous Psychokinesis (RSPK). Children seemed to attract such activity, and the Duke team discovered that Jimmy had been at or near the scene of the incidents most of the time.

When one of the researchers spent time with the boy—playing cards, helping him with his homework, or just talking—the unusual activity declined. Two more incidents occurred in early March before the Seaford Poltergeist apparently packed its bags and moved on. After 67 recorded incidents in five weeks, the lives of the Herrmann family returned to normal. To this day, it is still unknown exactly what caused the strange events in the Herrmann household in early 1958.

THE ROLLING HILLS ARE ALIVE WITH SPIRITS

You can turn an asylum into a mall, but you can't take the spirits out of it. That seems to be the case in East Bethany, New York, a small town located between Rochester and Buffalo. The main attraction there is a building that used to be a poorhouse and has undergone many changes during the nearly two centuries since it was constructed. However, it seems that its former residents just don't understand that the Rolling Hills Asylum is no longer their home.

THE POORHOUSE

Opened in 1827, the Genesee County Poorhouse was a residence for a wide array of people: Paupers, orphans, widows, and unwed mothers shared space with drunks, the mentally ill, the criminally insane, and the physically disabled. The massive structure served this eclectic group for 125 years before it was transformed into a nursing home in the 1950s.

Imagine the number of people who must have died there over the years. Some sources list the number of deaths at 1,750, but experts estimate that it was actually much higher. It's hard to say, though, because the dead were often dumped into unmarked graves.

In the early 1990s, the building was converted into a group of specialty shops known as Carriage Village. It wasn't long before store employees and shoppers began to notice some strange phenomena. When paranormal investigators were summoned, they observed mysterious shadows and doors that seemed to be held shut by an invisible force, as well as disembodied voices and screams. The property was officially declared "haunted." In 2003, the building was renamed Rolling Hills Country Mall, and the following year, it was opened to the public for ghost-hunting purposes and became known as "Rolling Hills Asylum."

BARGAIN HUNTERS GIVE WAY TO GHOST HUNTERS

Rolling Hills Country Mall has since closed its doors to shoppers, but in 2009, Sharon and Jerry Coyle purchased the property; they keep the building open as a paranormal research center, which hosts ghost tours and other special events.

Former owner Lori Carlson said that shadows and electronic voice phenomena (EVPs) are common occurrences at Rolling Hills, especially on the first and second floors of the East Wing—an area that was added to the building in 1958. Perhaps trying to avoid modern-day visitors, the spirits there seem to be most active between 3 a.m. and 5 a.m. And if you walk around the second floor of this wing, you might hear footsteps above you; the trouble is, the building has no third floor. The apparition of an older woman has been glimpsed heading into the ladies' room just outside the former cafeteria area; a man with a goatee has also been seen walking around the same area. And a former meat locker nearby is a good place to catch a few EVPs.

Another paranormal hot spot is the building's old solitary confinement cell, which was added in 1828 to house violent residents. These segregated souls frequently show themselves today.

SEE FOR YOURSELF

Rolling Hills Asylum attracts ghost hunters from all over the country, but working there isn't for the faint of heart. Staff member Suzie Yencer tells of one paranormal investigation during which the researcher wanted to try an experiment. The group gathered in a basement area known as the Christmas Room, where toys are often seen moving by themselves. No lights or detectors were used; the only illumination came from a pink glow stick that was set in the middle of the circle of people. Only Suzie was allowed to speak in the eerily quiet room: She was asked to try to make contact with the spirit world...and it worked. To her surprise, the glow stick moved back and forth, and a toy rocking horse in the room started to sway. Suzie and several others actually saw a phantom arm that appeared to reach for a ball; then, just as suddenly, it was gone.

In 2010, the *Ghost Adventures* team devoted an episode to the spirits of the old asylum. When Zak Bagans, Nick Groff, and Aaron Goodwin spent the night locked inside the old building, they heard disembodied voices and saw apparitions in their photos. Their experience, combined with the testimony of staff members and visitors, convinced them that Rolling Hills is a hotbed of paranormal activity.

Investigators from Central New York Ghost Hunters agreed. Members documented unexplained cold spots, phantom footsteps, hushed voices (which were captured on audio recorders), and actual physical contact, such as hair pulling and light taps or pokes.

THE NAUGHTY AND THE NICE

Visitors to Rolling Hills frequently report seeing the shadow of Roy, a former resident who suffered from gigantism, a disease that caused him to become unusually large. He grew to be over seven feet tall at a time when six feet tall was considered exceptionally large. Embarrassed by Roy's appearance, his parents left him at Rolling Hills in the late 1800s, when he was 12 years old; he lived there until he died at age 62. Roy was a gentle soul whose spirit emits friendly energy.But not every entity at Rolling Hills is as benevolent as Roy. Nurse Emmie Altworth was known to abuse patients and was thought to practice the dark arts and black magic. Inmates and other staff members feared her. Modern visitors have reported a feeling of evil and unease in the building's infirmary—possibly due to Emmie's negative energy.

If you visit Rolling Hills Asylum, watch out for its many spirits—the friendly and the anguished alike. And when you get home, be prepared to sleep with the lights on.

> "The death is not smooth. When there is trauma—an unacceptable accident or shock or surprise—this will, in some cases, cause the personality to go into a state of psychotic shock. In that state of shock, they are not aware that they've passed on. They are confused as to their real status because they can see everybody and nobody seems to be able to see them."
>
> **—Hans Holzer**

NEW JERSEY'S HAUNTED UNION HOTEL

A New Jersey hotel that witnessed a major event continues to make history of its own—haunted history, that is.

A SHOCKING EVENT

In early 1932, in an event that was as sad as it was sensational, Charles Lindbergh—the first man to fly solo across the Atlantic Ocean—again made headlines; however, this time it was for something that would have anything but a happy ending. On the night of March 1, 1932, the famous flyer's 20-month-old son was kidnapped from the family home in Hopewell, New Jersey. Although Lindbergh paid the requested ransom, the boy's body was eventually found half-buried in a roadside thicket not far from his home. Suspect Bruno Richard Hauptmann, a carpenter and small-time crook, was taken into custody on September 19, 1934. A transfixed American public anxiously awaited Hauptmann's trial, which was scheduled to begin on January 3, 1935, at the Hunterdon County courthouse in Flemington, New Jersey.

THE TRIAL OF THE CENTURY

Due to Lindbergh's fame and the revolting nature of the crime, the five-week proceeding was dubbed the "trial of the century." As such, it drew members of the press like moths to a flame. To keep reporters close to the action, the Union Hotel, which was located just across the street from the Hunterdon County courthouse, was tapped as the press headquarters. The Victorian building was an apt choice: Built in 1877, the four-story hotel was near the site of the trial, and it had a bar on its premises—just the thing to soothe battle-weary correspondents looking to unwind.

On February 13, 1935, the jury handed down a guilty verdict, which carried with it the death penalty. Happy that the villain had received his due, Americans rejoiced. Hauptmann went to the electric chair on April 3, 1936. Since that day, however, speculation regarding his culpability in the crime has stirred relentlessly. But that's not the only thing that's been stirring.

HARROWING HAPPENINGS

After the press departed the Union Hotel, little more was heard about the inn—little more of an *earthly* nature, that is. Staff reports of paranormal occurrences began trickling in, with each story sounding just a tad more terrifying than the one that preceded it. Over the years, several businesses have opened in the building—most recently a restaurant, which closed in 2008. According to witnesses, the ghosts of the Union Hotel have a penchant for vigorously spinning barstools. After this gets the attention of the intended eyewitness, which it unfailingly does, their next trick is to slam doors...loudly.

One night after closing, a bouncer locked the doors to the hotel's foyer and then joined staff members for a drink. Suddenly, the doors flew open—completely unaided— and a cold breeze blew past the group. Dumbfounded by what he had witnessed, the bouncer again closed the doors. As he did, he saw a phantom pair of children's shoes scrambling up the main stairway. Horrified, he turned and fled.

In another incident, a waitress was carrying her cash drawer upstairs after closing. As she reached the top step, she heard a disembodied voice humming a lullaby. Like the bouncer, she fled the scene, never to return again.

SPIRITS AND OTHER SPIRITS

At least one ghost at the Union Hotel has its disembodied heart in the right place. While going over her books late one night, a night manager sensed a sudden presence.

Startled, she moved back from her desk, and an invisible intruder moved up against her and pressed against her chest. She asked it to move away and the ghost respectfully complied. While some might categorize this turn of events as fortunate, the woman isn't so sure: She regrets telling the entity to back away for fear that she may never have such an encounter again.

Had the manager met the ghost of the condemned man? It's doubtful, since Hauptmann never stayed at the hotel. It's more likely that she brushed up against the spirit of a reporter left over from the days of the Hauptmann trial that was feeling a little frisky after unwinding in the bar.

THE UNHEALTHY MANSION

Violent, unexpected deaths are likely to produce ghosts, and shipwrecks are no exception. And when drowning deaths are combined with injustice, it's pretty much a given that a few restless spirits will remain earthbound. That was exactly the recipe for the haunting at the Mansion of Health.

THE HISTORY

Built in 1822, on New Jersey's Long Beach Island, the Mansion of Health was the largest hotel on the Jersey Shore upon its completion. This sprawling three-story structure featured a sweeping top-floor balcony that ran the length of the building and provided an unencumbered view of the glistening ocean, which was just a few hundred feet away. However, on April 18, 1854, the sea was anything but sparkling.

On that day, a violent storm turned the water into a foaming cauldron of death. Into this maelstrom came the *Powhattan,* a ship that was filled with more than 300 German immigrants who were bound for new lives in America. Unfortunately, the ship never had a chance. As it approached the coast of Long Beach Island, the storm tossed the boat onto the shoals and ripped a hole in its side. Passengers tumbled overboard, and later, dozens of bodies washed up on the shore.

STEALING FROM THE DEAD

Back in those days, a person known as a "wreck master" was responsible for salvaging cargo from shipwrecks and arranging the storage of those killed until the coroner took charge of their bodies. The wreck master for Long Beach Island was Edward Jennings, who was also the manager of the Mansion of Health. Accordingly, all of the bodies from the *Powhattan* that had come ashore were brought to the beach in front of the Mansion of Health.

When the coroner arrived hours later, he examined the bodies, although it didn't take a medical degree to determine that they had died from drowning. However, the coroner did find something peculiar: None of the dead had any money in their possession. It seemed unusual to him that immigrants who were coming to America to start new lives didn't carry any cash. Money belts were fashionable at the time, yet not a single victim was wearing one.

Suspicion immediately fell upon Jennings, who was the only person who'd had access to the bodies for many hours. However, no one had any proof of such a crime occurring, so the accusations died down.

THE LONG ARM OF THE GHOSTLY LAW

Four months later, another storm revealed a hole near the stump of an old tree on the beach near the Mansion of Health. In the hole, dozens of money belts were found; they were all cut open and empty.

When word of this discovery got out, Jennings took one look at the writing on the wall and hightailed it out of town, narrowly evading the long arm of the law. But there are some things that you can't escape, as Jennings found out the hard way. Supposedly, he became a broken man and was haunted by nightmares that destroyed his sleep and ruined his life. He died several years later in a barroom brawl in San Francisco.

However, the spirits of the *Powhattan* victims were not content to simply haunt Edward Jennings. Shortly after the accident, strange things began to happen at the Mansion of Health: Disembodied sobs were heard at night, and ghostly figures were seen walking across the hotel's expansive balcony. Guests also reported feeling uneasy, which is not exactly the best advertisement for a place that was supposed to be restful and encourage good health.

THE HAUNTED MANSION

Eventually, the Mansion of Health became known as the "Haunted Mansion," and people avoided it like the plague. Soon, the building was abandoned; the brooding hulk of a structure that towered over the beach slowly began rotting away.

During the summer of 1861, five young men who had more bravado than brains decided to spend the night in the gloomy structure. After cavorting through the empty halls and dashing around the balcony without seeing a single spirit, the men decided to sleep on the allegedly haunted third floor. After most of the young men had drifted off to sleep, one who remained awake suddenly noticed the luminous figure of a woman bathed in moonlight standing on the balcony; she held a baby in her arms. The apparition was gazing sadly out to sea, as if mourning the life that had been taken away from her so abruptly.

The startled young man quietly shook each of his companions awake, and all five gazed in disbelief at the figure. Each of them observed that the moonlight passed right through the woman. Then, suddenly and without warning, the woman vanished. The young men quickly gathered their belongings and fled the building, and from then on, not even vandals dared to enter the Haunted Mansion.

In 1874, fire destroyed the Mansion of Health. But the hotel's real end had come years earlier, when Edward Jennings made the unfortunate decision to tamper with the dead.

YALE'S SPIRITED ORGANIST

You know that an institution is rich with history when it is old enough to have celebrated its 300th anniversary in 2001. That's the case with Yale University, which opened its doors in New Haven, Connecticut, in 1701. While ghosts of students, professors, and even early colonists surely remain on these storied grounds, one particular area of Yale has quite a reputation for being haunted: Woolsey Hall.

Built in 1901—in recognition of the university's 200th anniversary—Woolsey Hall is the institution's main auditorium. It seats more than 2,500 people and has hosted performances by several symphonies, as well as rock concerts; but its ghosts aren't quite so fond of the latter.

The haunting of the building centers on the 1902 construction of the Newberry Memorial Organ—one of the largest and most renowned organs in the world. It is named for the Newberry family, which made a large donation to fund the instrument's upkeep. Harry B. Jepson, the school's first organist, played and maintained the pipe organ, but it periodically became outdated. The Newberry family stepped up to fund improvements to the organ in 1915 and 1928 to keep it state-of-the-art.

But in the 1940s, Yale forced Jepson to retire, and he never again played the Newberry Organ. While unhappy with this turn of events, the organist seemingly made peace with his situation—at least until the hall began hosting rock concerts. Some say that the last straw was when Jimi Hendrix played at Woolsey Hall on November 17, 1968. When Jepson's ghost saw this beautiful concert hall used for rock-and-roll music, he became angry.

Since that time, workers and visitors have reported feeling a menacing presence and a sense of evil in the hall, especially near the organ chambers and in the basement. People have heard the organ playing when the auditorium is locked and no one is sitting at the bench. One thing is certain: Jepson won't be playing any rock-and-roll music.

PENANCE FOR YOUR SINS

It started out as a unique way to help reform prisoners. It ended up being a literal torture chamber where men often died agonizing deaths. Sadly, too many of those tortured souls have been unable to leave the Eastern State Penitentiary—even in death.

THE ROAD TO PENANCE

The remains of the Eastern State Penitentiary—the location of a truly unique experiment in the history of law enforcement—stand on what is now Fairmount Avenue in Philadelphia. Designed by John Haviland, the facility was different from other prisons in that it was meant to stress reform rather than punishment. It was thought that by giving a prisoner plenty of time to reflect on his wrongdoing, he would eventually reform himself by turning to God to make penance—hence the word *penitentiary.*

In October 1829, when the Eastern State Penitentiary officially opened, it was one of the largest public buildings of its kind in the United States. And after its front gates swung open, its unique features blew prisoners and employees away. For starters, the entire complex resembled a giant wagon wheel, with seven wings of cells emerging from the center like spokes. The hallways themselves looked like the vestibules of a church.

ISOLATION AND MADNESS

Individual cells were designed to house only one inmate each. The idea was that prisoners needed time to reflect on what they had done wrong, and giving them cell mates would only distract them from doing that.

The only people with whom inmates were allowed to interact on a regular basis were the warden—who visited every prisoner once a day—and the guards—who served meals and brought inmates to and from their cells. Inmates were permitted to go outside for exercise, but they could only do that alone. When an inmate was removed from his cell for any reason, he was required to wear a hood. Prisoners were to remain silent at all times unless asked a direct question by prison personnel; failure to adhere to this rule meant swift, sadistic punishment.

TORTUROUS BEHAVIOR

The facility's initial intent may have been to get inmates to understand that they needed to follow the rules in order to be reformed, but that quickly broke down into brutality by the guards and officials. Minor offenses, including making even the smallest noise, were often enough for authorities to subject inmates to a series of hellish punishments. Restraint devices such as straitjackets and the "mad chair"—a chair equipped with so many restraints that it made even the slightest movement impossible—were often employed. If an inmate was caught talking, he might be forced to wear the "iron gag"—a piece of metal that was clamped to his tongue while the other end was attached to leather gloves that he was forced to wear; movement resulted in excruciating pain. Legend has it that several prisoners accidentally severed their own tongues while wearing the iron gag, and at least one died while wearing the device.

Another method of torture utilized at the Eastern State Pen was the water bath. Inmates were tied to the penitentiary walls and doused with freezing water, even in the middle of winter; under the most extreme conditions, the water would freeze on the inmates' bodies.

Perhaps one of the most heinous means of punishing an inmate was to place him in the "Klondike." While other prisons have "The Hole"—which is essentially solitary confinement—the Klondike at the Eastern State Pen was a group of four subterranean cells without windows or plumbing; inmates were made to live down there— often for several weeks at a time.

SWIFT DECLINE AND ABANDONMENT

The Eastern State Penitentiary was designed to change the world of incarceration in a positive way, but it failed miserably. In fact, when British author Charles Dickens visited the United States in 1842, one of the places that he wanted to see was the Eastern State Pen. From across the Atlantic, Dickens had heard about the marvelous and unique penitentiary and wanted to see it for himself. He was shocked by what he witnessed there, calling it "hopeless...cruel, and wrong."

Over the years, changes were enacted in an attempt to remedy the situation, but they didn't help. Finally, in 1971, the penitentiary was officially closed. In the mid-1990s, after sitting abandoned for years, the building was reopened for tours.

"NOT ALL WHO WALK THESE BLOCKS
ARE AMONG THE LIVING..."

Looking back at the tortuous history of the Eastern State
Pen, it should come as no surprise that more than a few
ghosts can be found there. In fact, records indicate that
inmates reported paranormal activity on the premises
as early as the 1940s, so it seems that ghosts were in
residence there long before the prison closed. Perhaps that
explains what happened to locksmith Gary Johnson while
he was working on a lock during a restoration of the prison
in the early 1990s. After Johnson popped the door open,
he saw shadowy shapes moving all around him. It was as
if he'd allowed all the ghosts to once again roam free.

If there's one area of the penitentiary where visitors are
most likely to experience paranormal activity, it is Cellblock
12. Many people have reported hearing voices echoing
throughout the cellblock and even laughter coming from
the cells themselves. Shadow figures are also seen in
abundance there.

Another location at the Eastern State Penitentiary that is
said to be haunted is the guard tower that sits high atop the
main wall. People standing outside the prison have seen
a shadowy figure walking along the wall; it calmly looks
down at them from time to time.

"DUDE, RUN!"

Over the years, various ghost-hunting television shows
have visited the Eastern State Penitentiary and submitted
paranormal evidence to their viewers. The facility was

featured in a 2001 episode of MTV's *Fear.* In 2007, *Most Haunted* investigated the place, and *Ghost Adventures* filmed an episode there in 2009. But if the Eastern State Penitentiary is forever linked to a paranormal research show, it would be *Ghost Hunters,* due to its team's 2004 investigation and the actions of one of its members.

At approximately 3 a.m., investigator Brian Harnois of The Atlantic Paranormal Society (TAPS) entered Cellblock 4 with Dave Hobbs, a member of the show's production crew. As Hobbs snapped a photograph, he and Harnois thought they saw a huge black shape rise up and move in front of them. They both panicked, and Harnois yelled out the now-famous line, "Dude, run!" after which the pair bolted down the hallway, much to the chagrin of their fellow investigators (who quickly deduced that the shape had been caused by the camera flash). The incident overshadowed an intriguing piece of evidence that was captured later that night, when one of the team's video cameras recorded a dark shape—almost human in form— that appeared to be moving quickly along a cellblock. Try as they might, TAPS was unable to come up with a scientific explanation for the shape, leaving who or what it was open to interpretation.

GET OUT OF JAIL FREE

If you would like to potentially encounter a ghost and have a firsthand look inside one of the truly unique architectural structures in the United States, the Eastern State Penitentiary is open for tours. You can also take part in a nighttime ghost tour there. Should you choose to embark on one of these adventures, be careful: A lot of the ghosts there are "lifers," and they just might jump at the chance to escape by following you home!

> "It is, alas, chiefly the evil emotions that are able to leave their photographs on surrounding scenes and objects, and whoever heard of a place haunted by a noble deed, or of beautiful and lovely ghosts revisiting the glimpses of the moon?"
>
> **—British author Algernon H. Blackwood**

GETTYSBURG'S GHOSTS

The Battle of Gettysburg holds a unique and tragic place in the annals of American history. It was the turning point of the Civil War and its bloodiest battle. From July 1 through July 3, 1863, both the Union and Confederate armies amassed a total of more than 50,000 casualties (including dead, wounded, and missing) at the Battle of Gettysburg. All that bloodshed and suffering is said to have permanently stained Gettysburg and left the entire area brimming with ghosts. It is often cited as one of the most haunted places in America.

FIRST GHOSTLY SIGHTING

Few people realize that the first sighting of a ghost at Gettysburg allegedly took place before the battle was over. As the story goes, Union reinforcements from the 20th Maine Infantry were nearing Gettysburg but became lost as they traveled in the dark. As the regiment reached a fork in the road, they were greeted by a man wearing a three-cornered hat, who was sitting atop a horse. Both the man and his horse appeared to be glowing. The man, who bore a striking resemblance to George Washington, motioned for the regiment to follow. Believing the man to be a Union general, Colonel Joshua Chamberlain ordered his regiment to follow the man. Just about the time Chamberlain starting thinking there was something odd about the helpful stranger, the man simply vanished.

As the regiment searched for him, they suddenly realized they had been led to Little Round Top—the very spot where, the following day, the 20th Maine Infantry would repel a Confederate advance in one of the turning points of the Battle of Gettysburg. To his dying day, Chamberlain, as well as the roughly 100 men who saw the spectral figure that night, believed that they had been led to Little Round Top by the ghost of George Washington himself.

DEVIL'S DEN

At the base of Little Round Top and across a barren field lies an outcropping of rocks known as Devil's Den. It was from this location that Confederate sharpshooters took up positions and fired at the Union soldiers stationed along Little Round Top. Eventually, Union soldiers followed the telltale sign of gun smoke and picked off the sharpshooters one by one.

After Devil's Den was secured by Union forces, famous Civil War photographer Alexander Gardner was allowed to come in and take photos of the area. One of his most famous pictures, "A Sharpshooter's Last Sleep," was taken at Devil's Den and shows a Confederate sharpshooter lying dead near the rocks. There was only one problem: The photograph was staged. Gardner apparently dragged a dead Confederate soldier over from another location and positioned the body himself. Legend has it that the ghost of the Confederate soldier was unhappy with how his body was treated, so his ghost often causes cameras in Devil's Den to malfunction.

PICKETT'S CHARGE

On July 3, the final day of the battle, Confederate General Robert E. Lee felt the battle slipping away from him, and in what many saw as an act of desperation, ordered 12,000 Confederate soldiers to attack the Union forces who were firmly entrenched on Cemetery Ridge. During the attack, known as Pickett's Charge, the Confederates slowly and methodically marched across open fields toward the heavily fortified Union lines. The attack failed miserably, with more than 6,000 Confederate soldiers killed or wounded before they retreated. The defeat essentially signaled the beginning of the end of the Civil War.

Today, it is said that if you stand on top of Cemetery Ridge and look out across the field, you might catch a glimpse of row after ghostly row of Confederate soldiers slowly marching toward their doom at the hands of Union soldiers.

JENNIE WADE

While the battle was raging near Cemetery Ridge, 20-year-old Mary Virginia "Ginnie" Wade (also known as Jennie Wade) was at her sister's house baking bread for the Union troops stationed nearby. Without warning, a stray bullet flew through the house, struck the young woman, and killed her instantly, making her the only civilian known to die during the Battle of Gettysburg. Visitors to the historical landmark known as the Jennie Wade house often report catching a whiff of freshly baked bread. Jennie's spirit is also felt throughout the house, especially in the basement, where her body was placed until relatives could bury her when there was a break in the fighting.

FARNSWORTH HOUSE

Though it was next to impossible to determine who fired the shot that killed Jennie Wade, it is believed that it came from the attic of the Farnsworth house. Now operating as a bed-and-breakfast, during the Battle of Gettysburg the building was taken over by Confederate sharpshooters. One in particular, the one who may have fired the shot that killed Jennie Wade, is said to have holed himself up in the attic. No one knows for sure because the sharpshooter didn't survive the battle, but judging by the dozens of bullet holes and scars along the sides of the Farnsworth house, he didn't go down without a fight. Perhaps that's why his ghost is still lingering—to let us know what really happened in the Farnsworth attic. Passersby often report looking up at the attic window facing the Jennie Wade house and seeing a ghostly figure looking down at them.

SPANGLER'S SPRING

As soon as the Battle of Gettysburg was over, soldiers began relating their personal experiences to local newspapers. One story that spread quickly centered on the cooling waters of Spangler's Spring. It was said that at various times during the fierce fighting, both sides agreed to periodic ceasefires so that Union and Confederate soldiers could stand side-by-side and drink from the spring. It's a touching story, but in all likelihood, it never actually happened. Even if it did, it doesn't explain the ghostly woman in a white dress who is seen at the spring. Some claim that the "Woman in White" is the spirit of a woman who lost her lover during the Battle of Gettysburg. Another theory is that she was a young woman who took her own life after breaking up with her lover years after the war ended.

PENNSYLVANIA HALL AT GETTYSBURG COLLEGE

One of the most frightening ghost stories associated with the Battle of Gettysburg was originally told to author Mark Nesbitt. The story centers around Gettysburg College's Pennsylvania Hall, which was taken over during the battle by Confederate forces, who turned the basement into a makeshift hospital. Late one night in the early 1980s, two men who were working on an upper floor, got on the elevator, and pushed the button for the first floor. But as the elevator descended, it passed the first floor and continued to the basement. Upon reaching the basement, the elevator doors opened. One look was all the workers needed to realize that they had somehow managed to travel back in time. The familiar surroundings of the basement had been replaced by bloody, screaming Confederate soldiers on stretchers. Doctors stood over the soldiers, feverishly trying to save their lives. Blood and gore were everywhere.

As the two men started frantically pushing the elevator buttons, some of the doctors began walking toward them. Without a second to spare, the elevator doors closed just as the ghostly figures reached them. This time the elevator rose to the first floor and opened, revealing modern-day furnishings. Despite repeated return visits to the basement, nothing out of the ordinary has ever been reported again.

A CONDEMNED MAN LEAVES HIS MARK

In 1877, Carbon County Prison inmate Alexander Campbell spent long, agonizing days awaiting sentencing. Campbell, a coal miner from northeastern Pennsylvania, had been charged with the murder of mine superintendent John P. Jones. Authorities believed that Campbell was part of the Molly Maguires labor group, a secret organization looking to even the score with mine owners. Although evidence shows that he was indeed part of the Mollies, and he admitted that he'd been present at the murder scene, Campbell professed his innocence and swore repeatedly that he was not the shooter.

THE SENTENCE

Convicted largely on evidence collected by James McParlan, a Pinkerton detective hired by mine owners to infiltrate the underground labor union, Campbell was sentenced to hang. The decree would be carried out at specially prepared gallows at the Carbon County Prison. When the prisoner's day of reckoning arrived, he rubbed his hand on his sooty cell floor then slapped it on the wall proclaiming, "I am innocent, and let this be my testimony!" With that, Alexander Campbell was unceremoniously dragged from cell number 17 and committed, whether rightly or wrongly, to eternity.

THE HAND OF FATE

Today, the Carbon County Prison not too different from the torture chamber that it was back then. Although it is now a museum, the jail still imparts the horrors of man's inhumanity to man. Visitors move through its claustrophobically small cells and dank dungeon rooms with mouths agape. When they reach cell number 17, many visitors feel a cold chill rise up their spine, as they notice that Alexander Campbell's handprint is still there!

"There's no logical explanation for it," says James Starrs, a forensic scientist from George Washington University who investigated the mark. Starrs is not the first to scratch his head in disbelief. In 1930, a local sheriff aimed to rid the jail of its ominous mark. He had the wall torn down and replaced with a new one. But when he awoke the following morning and stepped into the cell, the handprint had reappeared on the newly constructed wall!

Many years later Sheriff Charles Neast took his best shot at the wall, this time with green latex paint. The mark inexplicably returned. Was Campbell truly innocent as his ghostly handprint seems to suggest? No one can say with certainty. Is the handprint inside cell number 17 the sort of thing that legends are made of? You can bet your life on it.

THE HOOSAC TUNNEL

By the mid-1800s, the train was the preeminent form of transportation in America, and competition between railroad lines was fierce. If a means could be found to shorten a route, create a link, or speed up a journey, it was generally taken to help ensure a railroad's continued profitability.

A TRANSPORTATION MILESTONE

In 1848, the newly formed Troy and Greenfield Railroad proposed a direct route that would link Greenfield and Williamstown, Massachusetts. In Williamstown, it would connect to an existing route on which trains could travel to Troy, New York, and points west. The time-saving measure seemed like a brilliant move, except for one not-so-small detail: Between Greenfield and Williamstown stood a forbidding promontory known as Hoosac Mountain. In order to tame it, the railroad would need to drill a tunnel—but not just any tunnel: At nearly five miles in length, it would be the world's *longest* tunnel.

THE GREAT BORE

In 1851, the project was set in motion. Almost immediately, trouble arose when drillers learned that the soft rock stratum through which they were supposed to be boring was, in fact, harder than nails. In 1861, funding dried up, and by 1862—realizing that it had bitten off more than it could chew—the Troy and Greenfield Railroad defaulted on its loan. The state of Massachusetts stepped in to complete the tunnel.

With a steady infusion of cash and a government bent on completing the project, the Hoosac Tunnel was finally finished in 1873; in 1876, the "Great Bore" officially opened for business. The project had taken a quarter century to complete at a total cost of $21 million. Nearly 200 lives were lost while the tunnel was built, with 13 being the result of an incident that's legendary to this day.

TRAGEDY STRIKES

It happened on October 17, 1867, inside the tunnel's central shaft—a vertical hole that was drilled from atop the mountain to intersect with the midpoint of the tunnel 1,028 feet below. The shaft would supply much-needed ventilation to the tunnel and allow drillers two more facings from which to attack, a measure that would greatly speed up operations.

On this particular day, the shaft reached into the mountain some 538 feet. While attempting to light a lamp, a workman accidentally ignited a gasoline tank.

Within seconds, an inferno rocketed up to the surface, claiming the pumping station and hoist house located above, causing them to collapse into the deep pit. Unfortunately, 13 men were working in the shaft during the incident. As soon as was humanly possible, a miner was lowered into the smoldering cavity to search for survivors; he passed out during the long trip but managed to gasp "no hope" upon his return to the surface.

Without an operational pump, the cavity eventually filled to the brim with seepage and rainwater. It wasn't until a year later that the central shaft gave up its grisly contents. As it turns out, most of the victims hadn't died from the flames or from drowning: The stranded men had built a survival raft but were slowly asphyxiated by the poisonous gases and the oxygen-hungry flames raging above them.

SPIRITS RISE

In a 1985 article, Glenn Drohan—a reporter for the *North Adams Transcript*—told of strange phenomena at the tunnel, such as "vague shapes and muffled wails near the water-filled pit." Shortly after the accident occurred, workmen allegedly saw the spirits of the lost miners carrying picks and shovels. The workers called out to the missing men, but they did not answer, and their apparitions quickly vanished.

Other tragic goings-on at the Hoosac Tunnel include the strange death of Ringo Kelley. In 1865, when explosive nitroglycerin was first used for excavation, experts Kelley, Billy Nash, and Ned Brinkman attempted to set a charge of nitro before running for cover. Nash and Brinkman never made it: Kelley somehow set off the explosion prematurely, burying his coworkers in the process.

Shortly thereafter, Kelley vanished. He was not seen again until March 30, 1866, when his lifeless body was found two miles inside the tunnel. Bizarrely, he had been strangled to death at the precise spot where Nash and Brinkman had perished. Investigators never developed any leads, but workmen had an ominous feeling about Kelley's demise: They believed that the vengeful spirits of Nash and Brinkman had done him in.

PRESENT-DAY POLTERGEISTS

If the preceding tales seem quaint due to the passage of time, it's worth noting that the tunnel still features its share of hauntings; standouts among these are railroad worker Joseph Impoco's trio of supernatural tales. In an article that appeared in *The Berkshire Sampler* on October 30, 1977, Impoco told reporter Eileen Kuperschmid that he was chipping ice from the tracks one day when he heard a voice say, "Run, Joe, run!" As Impoco tells it, "I turned, and sure enough, there was No. 60 coming at me. Boy, did I jump back fast! When I looked [back], there was no one there."

Six weeks later, Impoco was working with an iron crowbar, doing his best to free cars that were stuck to the icy tracks. Suddenly, he heard, "Joe! Joe! Drop it, Joe!" He instinctively dropped the crowbar just as 11,000 volts of electricity struck it from a short-circuited power line overhead.

In the final incident, Impoco was removing trees from the tunnel's entrance when, from out of nowhere, an enormous oak fell directly toward him. He managed to outrun the falling tree, but he heard a frightening, ethereal laugh as he ran; he was certain that it hadn't come from any of his coworkers.

TRAVEL TIPS

For the brave at heart, a visit to the Hoosac Tunnel can prove awe-inspiring and educational. The tunnel is still used, so walking inside it is strictly off-limits, but a well-worn path beside the tracks leads to the Hoosac's entrance. For those who are looking to avoid things that go bump in the night, a trip to the nearby North Adams' Hoosac Tunnel Museum in the Western Gateway Heritage State Park will reveal the incredible history of this five-mile-long portal into another dimension—and will do so far away from Ringo Kelley's haunts. All aboard!

TORMENTED SPIRITS AT THE LIZZIE BORDEN B&B

Lizzie Borden took an ax and gave her mother 40 whacks, and when she saw what she had done, she gave her father 41.

This passage has been a schoolyard staple for more than a century; however, it contains a few errors. For example, it states that Lizzie Borden whacked her mother with an ax 40 times before turning on her father. In reality, the Bordens were murdered with a hatchet, not an ax. And Mrs. Borden

suffered around 20 wounds while her husband suffered
11—still more than enough to kill them both. What's more,
Abby Borden was Lizzie's stepmother, not her mother.
But the poem may have yet another inaccuracy:
Lizzie Borden may not have been the murderer at all!

"FATHER'S DEAD!"

Lizzie Borden grew up in Fall River, Massachusetts. In
1892, when the murders took place, Lizzie was still
living at home at age 32, which was old enough to be
considered a spinster by the standards of the day.

On August 4, 1892, the family's maid, Bridget Sullivan,
was in her upstairs room when she heard Lizzie screaming.
"Come down quick!" Lizzie shouted. "Father's dead!
Someone's come in and killed him!"

Andrew Borden was lying dead
on the couch, the victim of multiple
hatchet wounds. By some accounts,
he had been rolled over to look like
he was merely sleeping, but there was
blood everywhere.

While neighbors tended to the shocked Lizzie,
she was asked where she had been when all
of this happened. She replied that she had gone
to the barn to get something. A little while later,
the police found the body of Abby Borden in a
guest room. She was even more mutilated than
her husband.

Lizzie was the only person who the police ever arrested for the crime. A great deal of tension had existed between Lizzie and her father, for a variety of reasons. For example, Andrew's decision to divide his property among his relatives, rather than among his children, had caused much strife within the family. Also, he had recently killed Lizzie's pet pigeons, which he said had become a nuisance; he decapitated them and left the bodies for Lizzie to find.

Not long before the murders, Andrew had suspected that he was being poisoned. However, he didn't know who to accuse; after all, his miserly ways and shrewd business dealings had made him very unpopular in town—the culprit could have been almost anyone. But few people get poisoned simply for being unpopular, and Lizzie had been spotted buying cyanide at a local pharmacy just days before the murders. This made her look fairly suspicious.

In addition, Lizzie's explanation—that she had been in the barn while the murders took place—didn't convince everyone. For one thing, the bodies looked like they'd been moved. And how long could it possibly have taken her to get something out of the barn?

THE VERDICT

Lizzie was arrested for the murders, although the evidence against her was slim. There were no bloodstains on her dress when the police arrived on the scene, and no bloody clothes were ever found. A broken hatchet was located in the basement, but it could not be connected to the murders. With no solid evidence against Lizzie, the jury deliberated just 90 minutes before acquitting her.

After the trial, Lizzie changed her name to "Lizbeth" and went on with her life. She lived a somewhat lavish lifestyle in her new home, which she called Maplecroft, until her death in 1927.

Today, there are dozens of theories about the identity of the actual killer. Some say that it was Lizzie, while others think that it wasn't her but that she knew very well who it was. Still others believe that Lizzie had nothing to do with it. The sad truth is that we'll probably never know for sure who committed the crime. But the ghosts of Andrew and Abby Borden may want to keep the investigation alive.

CAN YOU STILL HEAR THE SCREAMS?

Years after the crime, the Borden House became a museum/bed-and-breakfast that was made to look almost exactly as it did at the time of the murders. Guests can actually sleep in the very room in which Abby Borden was killed and eat a breakfast of bananas, coffee, and johnnycakes, just like Mr. and Mrs. Borden did on that fateful morning before their brutal deaths.

Ghost sightings in the old green Victorian house are common—MSNBC even listed the house among the top ten most haunted houses in the United States.

The most active ghost there seems to be that of Abby Borden. Many guests have reported hearing the sound of a woman weeping in the bedroom where Abby's body was found. Many others have heard the sound of footsteps, and some have even reported that as they lay in their beds, an older woman in an old-fashioned Victorian-era dress has come into the room to tuck them in for the night.

But Abby is not the only ghost that roams the B & B. Guests have also occasionally spotted Andrew, and he has also manifested during séances that have been held at the house.

Lizzie's spirit has also been seen at the Borden home. From time to time, guests see a ghostly woman carrying a sharp weapon. Could this be Lizzie—or is it the real murderer?

Whoever they are, the ghosts at the Lizzie Borden Bed & Breakfast certainly aren't shy. Many guests have captured strange photos, videos, and audio recordings that feature unusual blobs of light, sounds resembling screams, and shadows that simply shouldn't be there. The owner of the house admits to being touched and pushed by unseen hands. And in 2008, a couple visiting on the anniversary of the brutal murders fled the B & B in terror after the door to their room flung open by itself and a lamp moved and lit up on its own. There are many haunted hotels around the world, but few generate as much paranormal activity as the Lizzie Borden Bed & Breakfast.

But allegedly, the Bordens don't just haunt their former home. People have seen mysterious lights at Oak Grove Cemetery, where the family is buried. And a few folks have even heard screams coming from the Borden plot, where Lizzie's body lies right next to the remains of her father and stepmother.

GHOSTS IN THE WITCH CITY

One of the darkest chapters in American history, the Salem Witch Trials have haunted our country for more than 300 years. Numerous plays and movies have recounted the tale of two young girls from Massachusetts who, in 1692, wrongfully accused people in their town of witchcraft. This sparked a mass hysteria that led to charges against hundreds and the executions of 20 innocent people. The lessons learned from this miscarriage of justice have stuck with the people of the United States, but so have the restless spirits of the victims of this tragedy.

THE LAST HOUSE

Today, the people of Salem, Massachusetts, acknowledge the crimes of the past, and the town recognizes its history in many ways, from witch logos on its police cars to a number of kitschy attractions erected solely to attract tourists. Among the gift shops and New Age bookstores, only one building with a connection to the trials remains: Known locally as "The Witch House," Judge Jonathan Corwin's former home still hosts visitors on Essex Street. Some of those visiting the historic site are overcome with feelings of anxiety, fear, and anger—all emotions likely experienced by those Corwin sentenced to death. Some have seen the apparition of a woman lingering in the bedrooms on the second floor, and others have witnessed a couple that vanishes into thin air while walking the grounds. Some employees report strange noises after hours, including what sounds like the shuffling of feet on the floorboards and the dragging of furniture from one room to another.

The spirits of The Witch House have even been captured on film, although most appear to be little more than manifestations of light or swirling mists.

THE GALLOWS

Judge Corwin's former home is not the only place in Salem where the spirits of those he condemned make their presence known. Photographs of orbs and mists that are similar to those snapped at The Witch House have been taken in the area once known as Gallows Hill. Though precise records of where the accused were hanged no longer exist, many believe that a playground and basketball court now reside where the town's gallows once stood. This would explain the eerie photographs of apparitions, as well as other strange phenomena that occur at the site. Electronics frequently malfunction there, and it isn't uncommon for people to hear otherworldly crying at the location at night. Some visitors have reported feeling an invisible presence brush up against them, while others have had their hair pulled by an unseen force.

HARBINGER AT HOWARD STREET

Of course, a town as old as Salem inevitably has several cemeteries, and one of the most haunted is Howard Street Cemetery, which sits across from where the old jail once stood. Photographers at the graveyard have captured images of the same unexplainable mists, orbs, and lights that are found at other locations, and reports of physical contact with an invisible entity abound as well. For more than a hundred years now, passersby have witnessed apparitions wandering among the old tombstones. Although most of the graves at the Howard Street Cemetery don't date back further than the 1800s, the site itself is inextricably tied to the witch trials: The graveyard was built on the location where Sheriff George Corwin tried to crush a confession out of Giles Corey—and when Corey's ghost is seen, the entire town of Salem trembles.

MORE WEIGHT...

When Anne Putnam accused Giles Corey of appearing to her as a spirit and trying to entice her with his satanic ways, Corey—who was over 80 years old at the time—didn't give the charge much credence. He even briefly supported accusations against his wife until he realized how seriously the charges were being taken. Sheriff Corwin, the son of Judge Jonathan Corwin, was getting rather wealthy

off the prosecution of so-called witches in Salem because anyone found guilty of witchcraft was subject to having his or her property seized and redistributed. That placed Giles Corey in a tough situation: If he pleaded guilty to the accusations against him, he would lose everything; at the same time, no one who had pleaded not guilty had been found to be innocent. Either outcome would mean that Corey's sons would not inherit his estate; instead, it would fall into the hands of the sheriff and the other town leaders. Corey did the only thing he could do: He refused to play their game.

COREY'S CURSE

Sheriff Corwin attempted to press a plea out of the old man—literally—by placing more and more weight on his chest every time he refused to confess, instead demanding, "More weight!" The act preserved his sons' inheritance but cost Giles Corey his life. Before he died, however, Corey spat at Corwin and sneered, "Damn you, Sheriff! I curse you and Salem!" Since then, sightings of Corey's ghost have meant disaster for the town. The last time he was spotted was in 1914, just before a fire that nearly wiped

Salem off the map. The curse doesn't only target the town itself, though: The very position that George Corwin once held is said to be cursed as well. Every sheriff of Salem since Corwin has either died in office or retired due to heart problems. Between the curse of Giles Corey and all the other restless spirits, one wonders why Salem hasn't changed its nickname from "The Witch City" to "The Haunted City."

CHAPTER 3

THE MIDWEST

A HAUNTING ON CHICAGO'S MAGNIFICENT MILE

Chicago's Water Tower stands more than 150 feet tall along the world-famous Magnificent Mile—one of the city's most popular tourist attractions. However, many visitors don't realize that the site is haunted by a hero who died there during the Great Chicago Fire of 1871.

MRS. O'LEARY LIT A LANTERN IN THE SHED

On the evening of October 8, 1871, the Great Chicago Fire began behind the O'Leary home. Contrary to popular belief, the fire was not started by a cow kicking over a lantern. Nevertheless, the flames spread quickly from the O'Leary barn.

When the smoke cleared a couple of days later, charred buildings and ashes littered the city. The fire had blazed a path nearly a mile wide and four miles long, leaving more than 100,000 people homeless.

Approximately 300 people died in the fire, but the heat was so intense that only 125 bodies were recovered. One of those bodies was a suicide victim found inside the Chicago Water Tower.

A HERO'S LAST RESORT?

According to legend, a lone fireman remained steadfast at the water-pumping station in Chicago's Streeterville neighborhood trying to save as many homes as possible. But as the flames closed in around him, he realized it was a losing battle. With his back to the Chicago Water Tower, there was no place to run.

As the fire edged closer, the brave fireman considered his options. Apparently, a slow death by fire seemed more frightening than a quicker end by his own hand. So the story goes that the fireman climbed the stairs inside the water tower, strung a rope from a beam near the top of the structure, and, in a moment of desperation, looped the rope around his neck and jumped to his death.

THE SOLITARY GHOST

The heat of the fire did not destroy the Chicago Water Tower, but it did scorch everything inside. The heroic fireman's identity was never known, but his spirit lingers. Hundreds of people have seen the sad figure of the hanging man and smelled a suggestion of smoke inside the tower, especially on October nights around the anniversary of the tragedy.

From outside the historic structure, some people see a pale man staring down at them from a window near the top of the tower. His expression is sad and resigned, and he seems to look right through those on the ground.

Other visitors have reported an eerie, sorrowful whistling that seems to come from inside the structure. It echoes through the tower, and then it stops abruptly.

However, most people who've seen the Water Tower ghost describe him with a rope around his neck, swinging and turning slowly. His face is twisted, grotesque, and highlighted as if flames are just beneath him. The ghost appears so real that many witnesses have called police to report a suicide. But responding officers, who have often seen the apparition themselves, know that he's a ghost… and a reminder of valor during a tragic fire more than a century ago.

THERE'S SOMETHING ABOUT MARY

Most big cities have their share of ghost stories, and Chicago is no exception. But beyond tales of haunted houses, spirit-infested graveyards, and phantom-filled theaters, one Chicago legend stands out among the rest: It's the story of a beautiful phantom hitchhiker of whom nearly everyone in the Windy City has heard. Her name is "Resurrection Mary," and she is Chicago's most famous ghost.

THE DEATH OF MARY

One version of the story says that Resurrection Mary was a young woman who died on Archer Avenue in Chicago's southwestern suburbs. On a cold winter's night in the early 1930s, Mary spent the evening dancing with her boyfriend at the Oh Henry Ballroom (known today as Willowbrook Ballroom) in Willow Springs, but when the evening ended with a quarrel between the two lovers, Mary decided to walk home. Tragically, she was killed when a passing car slid on the ice and struck her.

Mary's grieving parents buried her in Resurrection Cemetery, just down the road from the ballroom. She was reportedly wearing a fine white dress and dancing shoes when she was committed to eternity.

THE GIRL BY THE SIDE OF THE ROAD

Since that time, drivers have often witnessed a ghostly young woman standing on the side of the road near the gates of Resurrection Cemetery. Time and time again, motorists have reported picking up a pretty hitchhiker on Archer Avenue, only to see her disappear before letting her off. These accounts featured eerie similarities: In most cases, the woman was said to have blonde hair and wear a white party dress. The encounters almost always occurred near the ballroom or in the vicinity of Resurrection Cemetery.

Other reports took a more mysterious turn. Many young men claimed that they'd met a girl at a dance at the ballroom, spent the evening with her, and then offered her

a ride home at closing time. Her vague directions always
led them north along Archer Avenue until they reached
the gates of Resurrection Cemetery—where the girl would
inexplicably vanish from the car.

Although some drivers claimed that the mysterious woman
was looking for a ride, others reported that she actually
attempted to jump onto the running boards of their
automobiles as they drove past. And some even said that
they'd accidentally run over her outside the cemetery; when
they went to her aid, her body was gone. Others said
that their automobiles actually passed through the young
woman before she disappeared through the cemetery
gates.

Police and local newspapers fielded similar stories from
numerous frightened and frazzled drivers who had
encountered the ethereal young woman. These accounts
created the legend of "Resurrection Mary," as she came to
be known.

JERRY'S TALE

No Resurrection Mary story is as detailed or as harrowing
as that of Jerry Palus. He claimed to have met the
apparition at a Chicago dance hall in 1939. According
to Palus, the pair shared many spins around the dance
floor before the woman asked him for a ride home. She
asked him to take Archer Avenue, which he knew was
nowhere near the home address she had given him.
Nevertheless, he complied. When the car approached
Resurrection Cemetery, the woman asked Palus to pull over;
he couldn't understand why she'd want to be dropped off

in such a remote area. "This is where I have to get out," she explained in a soft voice, "but where I'm going, you can't follow." With that, the mysterious girl hurried toward the cemetery gates and vanished right before Palus's unbelieving eyes.

The next day, Palus visited the home address that the girl had given him. There, an older woman explained to him that he couldn't possibly have been with her daughter because she had been dead for several years. When Palus was shown a photo of the woman's daughter, his face turned pale as he realized that somehow, the young woman had come back from the grave to dance once again.

WILL THE REAL RESURRECTION MARY PLEASE STAND UP?

This legend has been told countless times over the years, and it may actually have some elements of the truth to it—but there may be more than one Resurrection Mary haunting Archer Avenue.

It is possible that in life, Resurrection Mary was a young Polish girl named Mary Bregovy. Mary loved to dance, especially at the Oh Henry Ballroom, and she was killed one night in March 1934 after spending the evening there and then downtown at some of the city's late-night clubs. She died along Wacker Drive in Chicago when the car in which she was riding collided with an elevated train support. Bregovy was buried in Resurrection Cemetery, and a short time later, a caretaker spotted her ghost walking through the graveyard. Stranger still, motorists on

Archer Avenue soon began telling stories of her apparition trying to hitch rides as they passed by the cemetery's front gates. For this reason, many believe that the ghost stories about Mary Bregovy may have given birth to the legend of Resurrection Mary.

However, as encounters with Resurrection Mary continued through the years, descriptions of the spectral girl have varied. Mary Bregovy had bobbed, light-brown hair, but most reports describe Resurrection Mary as having long blonde hair. So who could this ghost be?

Perhaps it's Mary Miskowski, who was killed along Archer Avenue in October 1930. According to sources, she also loved to dance at the Oh Henry Ballroom and at some other local nightspots. Many people who knew her in life believed that she might be the ghostly hitchhiker reported in the southwest suburbs.

In the end, we may never know Resurrection Mary's true identity, but there's no denying that sightings of her have been backed up with credible eyewitness accounts. In these reports, witnesses give specific places, dates, and times for their encounters with Mary—encounters that remain unexplained to this day. Mary is also one of the few ghosts that's ever left physical evidence behind.

BURNING DESIRE

Over the years, encounters with Resurrection Mary have been relatively common, but one account stands apart from all others. On August 10, 1976, a man driving past Resurrection Cemetery noticed a woman in a white dress standing inside the gates. She was grasping the metal bars of the gate, looking out toward the road. Thinking that she had been locked in, the driver notified the police. An officer responded to the call, but when he arrived at the cemetery, the girl was gone. He searched the location but found nothing out of the ordinary—until he glanced at the gate. It looked as though someone had pulled two of the bars with such intensity that small handprints were seared into the metal.

When word about the handprints got out, people from all over the area came to see them. Cemetery officials denied that anything supernatural had occurred, and they later claimed that the marks were created when a workman had tried to heat up the bars and bend them back into shape after a truck accidentally backed into the gate. It was a convenient explanation, but one that failed to explain the indentions that appeared to be left by small fingers and were plainly visible in the metal.

Cemetery officials were disturbed by this new publicity, so in an attempt to dispel the crowds of curiosity seekers, they tried to remove the marks with a blowtorch. However, this process made them even more noticeable, so the officials had the bars cut out and planned to straighten or replace them.

But removing the bars only made things worse, as people wondered what the cemetery was hiding. So the bars were put back into place, straightened, and then left alone so that the burned areas would oxidize and eventually resemble the other bars. However, the blackened areas did not oxidize, and the twisted handprints remained obvious until the late 1990s, when the bars were finally removed. At great expense, Resurrection Cemetery replaced the front gates, and the notorious bars were gone for good.

A BROKEN SPIRIT LINGERS ON

Sightings of Resurrection Mary aren't as frequent now as in years past, but they still persist, and many of them seem to be authentic. Many believe that Mary is on her way to her eternal resting place after one last night of dancing.

BACHELOR'S GROVE: AMERICA'S MOST HAUNTED CEMETERY?

Hidden away inside the Rubio Woods Forest Preserve near Midlothian, Illinois, lies Bachelor's Grove Cemetery, widely reported to be one of the most haunted cemeteries in the United States. Haunted or not, the cemetery certainly has an intriguing history that raises many questions but provides few answers.

Like almost everything associated with the cemetery, the very origins of Bachelor's Grove are surrounded in mystery. Some claim that the cemetery got its name in the early 1800s when several unmarried men built homes nearby, causing locals to nickname the area Bachelor's Grove. Others, however, believe the name was actually Batchelder's Grove, named after a family that lived in the area.

ABANDONED AND VANDALIZED

Despite its small size (about an acre), the cemetery became a popular site over the years because of its convenient location right off the Midlothian Turnpike. The quaint pond at the rear of the cemetery added to the allure, and as a result, about 200 individuals made Bachelor's Grove their final resting place.

All that changed during the 1960s when the branch of the Midlothian Turnpike that ran past the cemetery was closed, cutting it off from traffic. With the road essentially abandoned, people stopped coming to the cemetery altogether. The last burial at Bachelor's Grove took place in 1965, although there was an interment of ashes in 1989.

Without a proper road to get to the cemetery, Bachelor's Grove fell into a state of disrepair. Along with the cover of the Rubio Woods, this made the cemetery an attractive location for late-night parties and senseless vandalism. Today, of the nearly 200 graves, only 20 or so still have tombstones. The rest have been broken or gone missing. This, combined with rumors that some graves were dug up, is why many believe that the spirits of Bachelor's Grove do not rest in peace.

GLOW IN THE DARK

Who haunts Bachelor's Grove? For starters, the ghost of a woman dressed in white has been spotted late at night walking among the tombstones or sitting on top of them. So many people have seen her throughout the years that she is commonly known as the Madonna of Bachelor's Grove.

There are also reports of strange, flashing lights moving around the cemetery, especially near the algae-covered pond in the back. Some believe that the pond was used as an impromptu "burial ground" for Chicago-area gangsters and that the lights are the spirits of their victims. Others believe the strange orbs are related to the legend that, many years ago, a man plowing the nearby fields died when his horse became spooked and ran into the pond, drowning both man and horse.

Probably the most fascinating paranormal activity reported at Bachelor's Grove is that of the ghost house. On certain nights, a spectral house is said to appear in the distance along the abandoned road leading to the cemetery. Those who have witnessed this strange apparition say that the house slowly fades away until it disappears without a trace. Similarly, others have spotted a ghostly car barreling down the road, complete with glowing headlights.

Should you wish to visit Bachelor's Grove in the hopes of encountering some of these spirits, it is open every day but only during daylight hours. The abandoned road now serves as a well-worn path through the woods up to the cemetery. Just remember that you are visiting hallowed ground and the final resting places of men, women, and children. Be sure to treat it as such.

LINGERING SPIRITS OF THE *EASTLAND* DISASTER

The city of Chicago has a dark history of disaster and death, with devastating fires, horrific accidents, and catastrophic events. One of the most tragic took place on July 24, 1915. On that overcast, summer afternoon, hundreds of people died in the Chicago River when the Eastland *capsized just a few feet from the dock. This calamity left a ghostly impression on the Windy City that is still felt today.*

COMPANY PICNIC TURNS TRAGIC

July 24 was going to be a special day for thousands of Chicagoans. It was reserved for the annual summer picnic for employees of the Western Electric Company, which was to be held across Lake Michigan in Michigan City, Indiana. And although officials at the utility company had encouraged workers to bring along friends and relatives, they were surprised when more than 7,000 people arrived to be ferried across the lake on the five excursion boats chartered for the day. Three of the steamers—the *Theodore Roosevelt,* the *Petoskey,* and the *Eastland*—were docked on the Chicago River near Clark Street.

On this fateful morning, the *Eastland,* a steamer owned by the St. Joseph–Chicago Steamship Company, was filled to its limit. The boat had a reputation for top-heaviness and instability, and the new federal Seaman's Act, which was passed in 1915 as a result of the *Titanic* tragedy, required more lifeboats than previous regulations did. All of this resulted in the ship being even more unstable than it already was. In essence, it was a recipe for disaster.

DEATH AND THE *EASTLAND*

As passengers boarded the *Eastland,* she began listing back and forth. This had happened on the ship before, so the crew emptied the ballast compartments to provide more stability. As the boat was preparing to depart, some passengers went below deck, hoping to warm up on the cool, cloudy morning, but many on the overcrowded steamer jammed their way onto the deck to wave to onlookers on shore. The *Eastland* tilted once again, but this time more severely, and passengers began to panic. Moments later, the *Eastland* rolled to her side, coming to rest at the bottom of the river, only 18 feet below the surface. One side of the boat's hull was actually above the water's surface in some spots.

Passengers on deck were tossed into the river, splashing about in a mass of bodies. The overturned ship created a current that pulled some of the floundering swimmers to their doom, while many of the women's long dresses were snagged on the ship, tugging them down to the bottom. Those inside were thrown to one side of the ship when it capsized. Heavy furniture onboard crushed some passengers and those who were not killed instantly drowned a few moments later when water rushed inside. A few managed to escape, but most of them didn't. Their bodies were later found trapped in a tangled heap on the lowest side of the *Eastland.*

Firefighters, rescue workers, and volunteers soon arrived and tried to help people escape through portholes. They also cut holes in the portion of the ship's hull that was above the water line. Approximately 1,660 passengers survived the disaster, but they still ended up in the river, and many courageous people from the wharf jumped in or threw life preservers as well as lines, boxes, and anything that floated into the water to the panicked and drowning passengers.

In the end, 844 people died, many of them young women and children. Officially, no clear explanation was given for why the vessel capsized, and the St. Joseph–Chicago Steamship Company was not held accountable for the disaster. The bodies of those who perished in the tragedy were wrapped in sheets and placed on the *Theodore Roosevelt* or lined up along the docks. Marshall Field's and other large stores sent wagons to carry the dead to hospitals, funeral homes, and makeshift morgues, such as the Second Regiment Armory, where more than 200 bodies were sent.

After the ship was removed from the river, it was sold and later became a U.S. warship as the gunboat U.S.S. *Wilmette.* The ship never saw any action but was used as a training ship during World War II. After the war, it was decommissioned and eventually scrapped in 1947. The *Eastland* may be gone, but its story and ghosts continue to linger nearly a century later.

HAUNTINGS AT HARPO STUDIOS

At the time of the *Eastland* disaster, the only public building large enough to be used as a temporary morgue was the Second Regiment Armory, located on Chicago's near west side. The dead were laid out on the floor of the armory and assigned identification numbers. Chicagoans whose loved ones had perished in the disaster filed through the rows of bodies, searching for familiar faces, but in 22 cases, there was no one left to identify them. Those families were completely wiped out. The names of these victims were learned from neighbors who came searching for their friends. The weeping, crying, and moaning of the bereaved echoed off the walls of the armory for days.

The last body to be identified was Willie Novotny, a seven-year-old boy whose parents and older sister had also perished on the *Eastland*. When extended family members identified the boy nearly a week after the disaster took place, a chapter was closed on one of Chicago's most horrific events.

As years passed, the armory building went through several incarnations, including a stable and a bowling alley, before Harpo Studios, the production company owned by talk-show maven Oprah Winfrey, purchased it. A number of *The Oprah Show*'s staff members, security guards, and maintenance workers claim that the studio is haunted by the spirits of those who tragically lost their lives on the *Eastland*. Many employees have experienced unexplained phenomena, including the sighting of a woman in a long gray dress who walks the corridors and then mysteriously vanishes into the wall. Some believe she is the spirit of a mourner who came to the armory looking for her family and left a bit of herself behind at a place where she felt her greatest sense of loss.

The woman in gray may not be alone in her spectral travels through the old armory. Staff members have also witnessed doors opening and closing on their own and heard people sobbing, whispering, and moaning, as well as phantom footsteps on the lobby's staircase. Those who have experienced these strange events believe that the tragedy of yesterday is still manifesting itself in the old armory building's present state.

CHICAGO RIVER GHOSTS

In the same way that the former armory seems to have been impressed with a ghostly recording of past events, the Chicago River seems haunted, too. For years, people walking on the Clark Street bridge have heard crying, moaning, and pleas for help coming from the river. Some have even witnessed the apparitions of victims helplessly splashing in the water. On several occasions, some witnesses have called the police for help. One man even jumped into the river to save what he thought was an actual person drowning. When he returned to the surface, he discovered that he was in the water alone. He had no explanation for what he'd seen, other than to admit that it might have been a ghost.

So it seems that the horror of the *Eastland* disaster has left an imprint on this spot and continues to replay itself over and over again, ensuring that the unfortunate victims from the *Eastland* will never truly be forgotten.

CHICAGO'S ORIENTAL THEATRE IS NEVER COMPLETELY EMPTY

When Chicago's Iroquois Theatre opened for business, one patron is known to have described the place as "a death trap." However, according to records, the building was fully in compliance with the fire code, and advertisements billed it as "absolutely fireproof." Unfortunately, that first description proved to be true.

FALSE ADVERTISING

When the Iroquois Theatre opened in November 1903, it was easy to feel safe while sitting underneath its ornate, 60-foot-high ceiling and among its white marbled walls and grand staircases. But, unbeknownst to patrons, when the theater was under construction, its owners had cut corners to open in time for the 1903 holiday season.

In retrospect, it's easy to wonder if the owners of the Iroquois were purposely inviting trouble. After all, they had declined to install sprinkler systems, and not all of the fire escapes were completed when the theater opened. In addition, exit signs were either missing or obscured by thick drapes, there were no backstage phones or fire buckets, and no fire alarm system was in place; in fact, the only fire-fighting equipment in the theater was a few canisters of a chemical product called Kilfyre. The owners had even skimped on the stage's safety curtain: Instead of using fireproof asbestos to make it, the owners saved about $50 by having the builders use a blend of asbestos, cotton, and wood pulp. But at the time, it was not uncommon for building inspectors and city officials to accept bribes to look the other way as builders ignored one safety law after another.

"A DEATH TRAP"

On December 30, barely a month after the theater opened, vaudeville star Eddie Foy and his company were onstage performing the musical *Mr. Blue Beard* to a standing-room-only crowd that was estimated to be around 2,000 people—a few hundred more than the theater could safely hold.

At the beginning of the second act, a calcium light arced and sent a spark onto a muslin drape on a wall near the stage. The orchestra stopped playing, but Foy urged the audience to remain calm and stay in their seats. Even after the flames jumped to pieces of scenery that were hanging in the rafters—most of which were painted with highly flammable oil-based paint—Foy stayed onstage and begged the audience to remain calm and exit the theater in an orderly fashion. But Foy was no fool: He knew that when the scenery in the rafters caught fire, the situation was going to get a lot worse.

Above and behind him, the fire spread quickly, and the cast and crew dashed for a backstage exit. Lighting gear jammed the fire curtain after it dropped only a few feet, which left the audience fully exposed to the flames on the stage.

Unbeknownst to the performers who scrambled to open the back door, the owners had ordered the ventilation system nailed shut. This kept the cold December air from getting inside, but it also effectively turned the building into a gigantic chimney. The minute the door was opened, a back draft turned the flames on stage into what eyewitnesses described as a "balloon of fire." This massive fireball shot through the auditorium, incinerating some people right where they stood.

Naturally, the crowd panicked and ran for the fire exits, which the owners had locked to keep people from sneaking into the theater without paying. Those who weren't trampled trying to reach the fire exits ran for the front doors, hoping to rush out onto Randolph Street. But the doors opened in toward the lobby, not out toward the street, so rather than escaping through the doors, the people crashed into them, and then into each other. More people died from being crushed in the melee than from burns or smoke inhalation.

Meanwhile, the only hallway that led downstairs from the balcony was blocked by a metal accordion gate—which was placed there to keep people from sneaking into better seats—effectively trapping the unfortunate people in the upper reaches of the burning building. Some tried to jump from the balcony to escape; others opened the balcony's fire exit, which was miraculously kept unlocked. However, by the time those who opened the door realized that there *was* no fire escape behind the door, the crowd was pushing too hard for them to turn back: They were shoved out the door and dropped nearly 60 feet into the alley below. By the time the situation had calmed down, more than a hundred people had fallen to their demise in what newspapers called "Death Alley."

IN THE WAKE OF TRAGEDY

The exact number of lives lost in the Iroquois Theatre fire is uncertain. Around 600 people are known to have perished—which is twice the number that died in the Great Chicago Fire of 1871—but the actual number is probably much higher because some families picked up their dead before they could be counted. To this day, the fire at the Iroquois Theatre is the deadliest single-building fire in U.S. history. But on the positive side, steel fire curtains, clearly marked exits, and exit doors that swing out toward the street are all provisions that were mandated because of the Iroquois tragedy.

Following the incident, a number of city officials were brought to trial for gross negligence, but they all got off on technicalities. The only people ever successfully prosecuted for crimes surrounding the Iroquois fire were a few of the crooks who broke into the theater to shimmy rings off fingers, yank necklaces from necks, and dig money out of the pockets of the deceased (and the vast majority of these people were never prosecuted, either).

THE BUILDING MAY BE GONE,
BUT THE GHOSTS REMAIN

Ghost sightings at the Iroquois Theatre began before the flames had even stopped smoldering: Photographs taken of the ruined auditorium shortly after the fire contain strange blobs of light and mist that some believe are the spirits of the unfortunate victims.

The theater was soon repaired and reopened, and it operated under various names for another 20 years before it was torn down. In its place, a new venue—the Oriental Theatre—was erected in 1926. For years, it was one of Chicago's premier movie theaters until it fell on hard times in the 1970s, when it mainly played kung fu movies. The Oriental Theatre finally shut its doors in 1981, and it seemed as though the Iroquois and its tragic tale had faded into Chicago's history.

But since 1998, when the Oriental Theatre reopened to host touring Broadway shows, employees have found that the ghosts have stuck around. During rehearsals, spectators are frequently seen in the balcony seats. When staff members are sent to ask them to leave, they find the balcony empty.

Many people who work in the building have reported seeing the specter of a woman in a tutu. This is thought to be the ghost of Nellie Reed, an aerialist who was in position high above the audience when the fire broke out. Although she was rescued from her perch, she suffered severe burns and died a few days later.

Other actors and crew members have encountered the ghost of a young girl who makes her presence known by giggling and flushing one of the toilets backstage. Her happy laugh has been picked up on audio recorders on more than one occasion and can often be heard in the hallways next to the main auditorium.

Staff members who work late at night, after all of the theatergoers have left the building, have reported seeing shadowy blobs that they call "soft shapes." These mysterious forms are seen zipping through the empty auditorium toward the places where the fire exits would have been in 1903.

And the ghosts in the theater may not only be spirits from the fire; female staff members have reportedly been harassed and threatened by a strange male voice in one of the sub-basements located far below the street. Historians suggest that this ghost may be from the 19th century, when the section of Randolph Street where the theater now stands was known as "Hairtrigger Block" and was home to the rowdiest gambling parlors in town.

Sometimes, when a building is torn down, its ghosts seem to go away. But other times, as seems to be the case with the Iroquois Theatre, they only get louder and more active.

> "It struck me as I looked out over the crowd during the first act that I had never seen so many women and children in the audience."
>
> —**Eddie Foy,** who witnessed the Iroquois fire firsthand

THE GHOSTS OF THE
ST. VALENTINE'S DAY MASSACRE

After Chicago gangsters lured their rivals into an ambush, they thought that they had enjoyed the last laugh. What they failed to consider was the existence of another syndicate—one from the Other Side.

REQUIEM FOR RACKETEERS

During the Roaring '20s, Al "Scarface" Capone ruled Chicago. Be it gambling, prostitution, bootleg whiskey, or anything else illegal or immoral, Capone and his gangsters controlled it. Almost no one—including the police—dared to stand up to Capone and his men because resistance certainly meant winding up on the wrong end of a gun. Still, one man was determined to dethrone Capone: George "Bugs" Moran.

Moran and his North Side Gang had been slowly muscling their way into Chicago in an attempt to force Capone and his men out. As 1929 began, rumors indicated that Capone was planning to "take care of" Moran. As the days turned into weeks and nothing happened, Moran and his men began to relax and let their guard down. That would prove to be a fatal mistake.

GATHERING FOR THE SLAUGHTER

On February 14, 1929, six members of the North Side Gang gathered inside the SMC Cartage Company at 2122 North Clark Street. With them was mechanic John May, who was not a member of the gang but had been hired to work on a member's car. May had brought along his dog, Highball, and had tied him to the bumper of the car while he worked. At approximately 10:30 a.m., two cars parked in front of the Clark Street entrance of the building. Four men—two dressed as police officers and two in street clothes—got out and walked into the warehouse.

MURDERERS IN DISGUISE

Once the men were inside, it is believed they announced that the warehouse was being raided and ordered everyone to line up facing the back wall. Believing that the uniformed men were indeed police officers, all of Moran's men, along with John May, did as they were told. Suddenly, the supposed raiders began shooting, and in a hail of shotgun fire and more than 70 submachine-gun rounds, the seven men were brutally murdered.

After the slaughter was over, the two men in street clothes calmly walked out of the building with their hands up, followed by the two men dressed as police officers. To everyone nearby, it appeared as though a shootout had occurred and that the police had arrived and arrested two men.

"NOBODY SHOT ME"

Minutes later, neighbors called police after hearing strange howls coming from inside the building. When the real police arrived, they found all seven men mortally wounded. One of the men, Frank Gusenberg, lingered long enough to respond to one question. When authorities asked who shot him, Gusenberg responded, "Nobody shot me." The only survivor of the melee was Highball the dog.

When word of the massacre hit the newswire, everyone suspected that Al Capone had something to do with it. Although Capone swore that he wasn't involved, most people felt that he had orchestrated the whole thing as a way to get rid of Moran and several of his key men. There was only one problem: Bugs Moran wasn't in the warehouse at the time of the shooting. Why he wasn't there is not clear, but one thing is certain: February 14, 1929, was Bugs Moran's lucky day.

Police were unable to pin anything related to the crime on Capone, although they did charge two of his gunmen— John Scalise and Jack "Machine Gun" McGurn—with the murders. Scalise never saw the inside of the courthouse: He was murdered before his trial began. Charges against McGurn were eventually dropped; however, he was murdered seven years later—on Valentine's Day—in what appeared to be retaliation for the 1929 massacre.

HAUNTED BY THE TRUTH

Publicly, Al Capone may have denied any wrongdoing, but it appears that the truth literally haunted him until his dying day. In May 1929, Capone was incarcerated at Philadelphia's Eastern State Penitentiary, serving a one-year stint for weapons possession. Such a span was considered "easy time" by gangster standards, but Capone's time inside would be anything but. Haunted by the ghost of James Clark—who was killed in the St. Valentine's Day Massacre—Capone was often heard begging "Jimmy" to leave him alone.

The torment continued even after Capone was released. One day, Capone's valet, Hymie Cornish, saw an unfamiliar man in Capone's apartment. When he ordered the man to identify himself, the mysterious figure slipped behind a curtain and vanished. Capone insisted that Cornish, like himself, had seen the ghost of Clark. Some say that Clark didn't rest until Capone passed away on January 25, 1947.

GHOSTS STILL LINGER

Over the years, the warehouse in which the St. Valentine's Day Massacre took place transformed into a morbid tourist attraction, as curiosity seekers felt compelled to see the site for themselves. When the building was demolished in 1967, the wall against which the seven doomed men stood was dismantled brick by brick and sold at auction. An enterprising businessman purchased the bricks and eventually sold each one, but many of them were returned soon after. According to unhappy customers, their luck took a nosedive after they purchased the ghoulish souvenirs. Illness, financial ruin, divorce, and even death caused the frightened owners to believe that the bricks were cursed.

As for the infamous massacre site, nothing much is left there today. A nursing home owns the land and has left the area vacant, save for a parking lot and a few trees. Some people have reported hearing gunfire and screams as they pass by the site; and people walking their dogs near the lot claim that their furry friends pull on their leashes and try to get away from the area. Perhaps they sense the ghostly remnants of the bloody slaughter that took place there so many years ago.

THE WATSEKA WONDER: A TALE OF POSSESSION

Spiritual possession—in which a person's body is taken over by the spirit of another—is easy to fake, and legitimate cases are incredibly rare. One of the most widely publicized possessions occurred in Watseka, Illinois, in the late 1870s, when the spirit of Mary Roff, a girl who had died 12 years earlier, inhabited the body of 13-year-old Lurancy Vennum. This astounding case became known as the "Watseka Wonder."

A TROUBLED LIFE

In 1865, Mary Roff was just 18 years old when she died in an insane asylum following a lifelong illness that tormented her with frequent fits, seizures, and strange voices in her head. She'd also developed an obsession with bloodletting and would apply leeches to her body, poke herself with pins, and cut herself with razors. Doctors thought that Mary was mentally ill, but others—including her own family—came to believe that her problems were supernatural in origin.

At the time of Mary Roff's death, Lurancy Vennum was barely a year old. Born on April 16, 1864, Lurancy moved with her family to Watseka a few years after Mary Roff's death and knew nothing of the girl or her family.

In July 1877, about 12 years after Mary passed away, Lurancy started to exhibit symptoms similar to Mary's, including uncontrollable seizures. Her speech became garbled, and she often spoke in a strange language. She sometimes fell into trances, assumed different personalities, and claimed to see spirits, many of which terrified her.

The townspeople of Watseka didn't know what to make of Lurancy. Many thought that she was insane and should be committed, as Mary had been. But the Roffs, who had become ardent Spiritualists as a result of their daughter's troubles, believed that unseen forces were tormenting Lurancy. They felt that she was not insane but rather was possessed by the spirits of the dead. With the permission of Lurancy's parents, Asa Roff—Mary's father—met with the young girl in the company of Dr. E. Winchester Stevens, who was also a Spiritualist. During their visit, a friendly spirit spoke to Lurancy and asked to take control of her body to protect her from sinister forces. That spirit was Mary Roff.

SENT TO HEAVEN

After Mary took possession of Lurancy's body, she explained that Lurancy was ill and needed to return to heaven to be cured. Mary said that she would remain in Lurancy's body until sometime in May. Over the next few months, it seemed apparent that Mary's spirit was indeed in control of Lurancy's body. She looked the same, but she knew nothing about the Vennum family or her life as Lurancy. Instead, she had intimate knowledge of the Roffs, and she acted as though they were her family. Although she treated the Vennums politely, they were essentially strangers to her.

In February 1878, Lurancy/Mary asked to go live with her parents—the Roffs. The Vennums reluctantly consented. On the way to the Roff home, as they traveled past the house where they'd lived when Mary was alive, Lurancy wanted to know why they weren't stopping. The Roffs explained that they'd moved to a new home a few years back, which was something that Lurancy/Mary would not have known. Lurancy/Mary spent several months living in the Roff home, where she identified objects and people that Lurancy could not have known.

On one occasion, Lurancy sat down at the Roff's family piano and began to play, singing the same songs Mary had sung in her youth. One member of the Roff family commented, "As we stood listening, the familiar [songs] were hers, though emanating from another's lips."

Once word spread of Lurancy's spiritual possession, interested people started to visit. Lurancy/Mary typically met them in the Roffs' front parlor, where she frequently demonstrated knowledge of events that had transpired long before Lurancy was even born.

During one encounter with a Mrs. Sherman, Mary was asked about the people she had met in the afterlife. Immediately, Mary started listing the names of some of Mrs. Sherman's deceased family members, as well as several of

Mrs. Sherman's neighbors who had died. Again, this was information that Lurancy could not possibly have known.

SCENE AT A SÉANCE

In April 1878, during a séance that was held in the Roff home and attended by several people (including Dr. Stevens), one member of the group became possessed by the spirit of another member's dead brother, who addressed the gathering. After the spirit had left the man's body, Mary removed herself from Lurancy's body (which immediately lolled over against the person next to her, as if dead) and possessed the body of a participant named Dr. Steel. Through him, Mary proved to everyone present that it was indeed her. She then abandoned Dr. Steel's body and reentered Lurancy's.

GOING HOME

Mary permanently left Lurancy's body on May 21, 1878. When Lurancy awoke from her trance, she was no longer afflicted by the numerous problems that had previously plagued her, nor did she have any recollection of being spiritually possessed by Mary. By all accounts, she came away from the experience a healthy young lady. Indeed, Lurancy grew to be a happy woman and exhibited no ill effects from the possession. She went on to marry and have 13 children.

But Mary didn't abandon Lurancy completely. According to some sources, Lurancy kept in touch with the Roff family, with whom she felt a strange closeness, although she had no idea why. She would visit with them once a year and allow Mary's spirit to possess her briefly, just like it did in the late 1870s.

The story of the Watseka Wonder still stands as one of the most authentic cases of spirit possession in history. It has been investigated, dissected, and ridiculed, but to this day, no clear scientific explanation has ever been offered.

ROGUES' HOLLOW

Coal miners lived a hard life in the 19th century. Most of the digging was done by hand, and they had to live with everyday hazards such as poor ventilation, cave-ins, and machinery accidents. As a result, miners not only worked hard, but they played hard, as well. And when they wanted to play, they went to Rogues' Hollow.

THE HISTORY

In the 1820s, Doylestown, Ohio, was a quiet place to live, with most of its citizens being farmers—that is, until coal was discovered in the area. Soon people from all over came to work in the coal mines that sprung up around town. By the time the coal industry left the area in the 1940s, more than 50 coal mines had operated in the area. Originally, Rogues' Hollow consisted only of a store or two, a mill, and a single saloon just southeast of Doylestown. In order to meet the thirsty needs of the miners, more saloons opened up. And while most had tame names such as Smith's Saloon, several bore more foreboding monikers, including the infamous Devil's Den, run by Billy Gallagher. The bloodiest fights to take place in the Hollow were said to have started in the Devil's Den.

For those who weren't in the mood for their own fight, customers could head across the street to Walsh's Saloon to watch (and bet on) illegal cockfights that took place every night. Often the betting would get so fierce that drunken patrons would rip dollar bills in half and try to make 50-cent bets. But as rowdy as things got inside Walsh's, everyone knew to give the owner, Mike Walsh, a wide berth: He struck a hulking figure at more than 300 pounds and needed two "normal-size" chairs to sit comfortably.

MURDER AND MAYHEM

Surprisingly, the number of deaths inside Rogues' Hollow proper was quite low, but the number of disappearances was quite high. In most cases, miners simply picked up and moved to another town. In other cases, drunken miners took a wrong turn while stumbling home drunk and met a swift death by falling into a mine shaft—in fact, quite a number of bodies were discovered at the bottom of mine shafts. Whispers throughout the town claimed that some of those accidental deaths were really murders.

Wanted criminals often hid out in the Hollow, and even the bravest officer of the law refused to enter the town. Moreover, the abandoned mines that riddled the countryside were fantastic places for men to hole up... literally. One famous criminal often associated with Rogues' Hollow is Richard Hulett of Akron, who was arrested and charged with counterfeiting large amounts of half-dollars and dollars in November 1893. While Hulett was convicted, he never gave up the location of his counterfeiting operation, leading many to believe Hulett had set up shop in one of the Hollow's abandoned mines. One long-standing legend even claims that Jesse James himself hid in the Hollow for a few days.

THE GHOSTS OF ROGUES' HOLLOW

With all the violence and death that took place in Rogues' Hollow, it would stand to reason that the place would be home to more than a few restless spirits. Perhaps the most famous is the ghost said to haunt Chidester's Mill. The wool mill owned and run by Samuel Chidester had been operating in Rogues' Hollow for several years when, according to legend, a young boy working there was accidentally crushed to death. Today, his ghost is said to still wander the long-since silent remains of the mill.

Several other reports of spooky activity in Rogues' Hollow include ghostly figures in white as well as picks and axes that "dance" on their own. Of course, since there was so much drinking going on in Rogues' Hollow, one wonders if what the witnesses saw was the result of spirits from inside a bottle rather than spirits from the Other Side. Today, little remains from the rough-and-tumble era of Rogues' Hollow save for a few buildings. But curiosity seekers and history buffs can still visit the area, which is maintained by the Chippewa-Rogues' Hollow Historical Society, and, just maybe, the restless spirits of 19th-century miners.

THE HAUNTED CASTLE OF MANSFIELD, OHIO

As you turn onto Reformatory Road in Mansfield, Ohio, you can't help but gasp as you gaze upon the immense castlelike structure that looms before you. As we all know, every good castle needs at least one resident ghost, and the Mansfield Reformatory doesn't disappoint in that regard.

FROM CAMP TO CASTLE

During the Civil War, the property on which the Mansfield Reformatory now stands was the site of Camp Mordecai Bartley. After the war, the decision was made to construct a reformatory there that would function as a sort of middle ground for first-time offenders, allowing only hardened criminals and repeat offenders to be sent to the Ohio Penitentiary in Columbus. But the Mansfield Reformatory would be no ordinary structure—it would be an imposing edifice designed to strike fear into the heart of any prisoner forced to enter its massive gates.

In the 1880s, architect Levi T. Scofield began designing the reformatory. The entire front portion would house the warden, his family, and the administrative offices; the rear portion would contain the massive six-tier cellblock, which would be the tallest freestanding cellblock in the world.

Incredibly, when the Mansfield Reformatory finally opened in September 1896, the 150 inmates transferred there entered a building that still wasn't complete. In fact, the prisoners themselves were responsible for finishing the construction, a task that included completing a giant wall surrounding the main building. The structure would not be fully finished until 1910.

CRAMPED QUARTERS AND VIOLENCE

It doesn't seem possible that such a massive building could become overcrowded, but that's exactly what happened: By 1930, the reformatory was already well over capacity. In fact, inmates were often sleeping three or four to a cell that was designed to fit only two.

The cramped quarters may have been one reason why prisoners at the Mansfield Reformatory were so aggressive. Considering the fact that the facility did not house hardened criminals, the amount of violence that took place there is staggering. A riot in 1957 involved more than 100 inmates. There were also a few instances in which one inmate killed another. Several prisoners couldn't take the living conditions and committed suicide, including one man who set himself on fire. Eventually, word of the horrible conditions reached the public, and in the early 1980s, officials declared the Mansfield Reformatory unfit to continue functioning as a prison; it would be another ten years before the facility was actually shut down.

The building seemed destined for the wrecking ball until Hollywood came calling in the early 1990s, when the majority of *The Shawshank Redemption* (1994) was filmed at the former prison. Not long after, the Mansfield Reformatory Preservation Society was formed. One of the first items on the group's agenda was to open the building for overnight ghost tours. After that, people from all walks of life started to come face-to-face with spirits from the Other Side.

HAUNTED BY THE PAST

One of the most enduring ghost stories associated with the Mansfield Reformatory centers on Warden Arthur L. Glattke and his wife, Helen. In 1950, Helen was getting ready for Sunday mass when she went into a closet in the warden's quarters to retrieve a box from a high shelf. As she grabbed the box, she bumped a revolver that Arthur had hidden in the closet; the gun went off and wounded her. She was rushed to the hospital, but she died several days later of pneumonia while recovering from her injury.

On February 10, 1959, Arthur was working in his office when he suffered a fatal heart attack. Almost immediately, rumors began to suggest that Helen's death had not been an accident, but rather that Arthur had killed her and made it look like an accident. Further, it was said that Arthur's heart attack was the result of Helen's ghost exacting its revenge. It's a creepy story, but it can't be proven. In fact, by all accounts, the couple truly loved each other. Perhaps that's why when people see the ghosts of the couple, they appear happy as they walk up and down the hallways of the warden's quarters.

INVESTIGATING THE REFORMATORY

While the Mansfield Reformatory had been featured on numerous television shows such as *Scariest Places on Earth*, it wasn't until The Atlantic Paranormal Society (TAPS) visited in 2005 for *Ghost Hunters* that people everywhere got a look at a paranormal investigation inside the prison's walls.

During that investigation, TAPS members heard strange footsteps echoing throughout the prison; they also managed to videotape unexplained lights at the far end of the hallway in solitary confinement. But the most intriguing part of the evening came when investigators Dustin Pari and Dave Tango were walking on the second floor of the East Cellblock. The duo heard strange noises coming from one of the cells, but when they were unable to find the source of the sounds, they marked an "X" outside the cell so they could find it later. About an hour later, investigators Jason Hawes and Grant Wilson were in the same area when Hawes thought that he saw something moving inside the cell marked with an "X," and Wilson believed he heard something there. However, upon investigating the cell, it appeared to be empty.

DOING TIME WITH THE GHOSTS

You don't have to be on a reality TV show to experience the unknown at Mansfield Reformatory. Over the years, paranormal research group The Ghosts of Ohio has spent several nights locked inside the prison. Each time, group members have witnessed strange phenomena, including hearing disembodied footsteps in the hallways, seeing shadowy figures moving in the cellblocks, having equipment malfunction, and experiencing feelings of heaviness while in Solitary Confinement.

The Mansfield Reformatory currently offers tours, so you can see for yourself if anything supernatural is lurking there. But if you're not lucky enough to spot the Glattkes, fear not: Plenty of other ghosts are said to lurk inside the old prison. So if you dare, head to Solitary Confinement, where people report experiencing cold chills, feeling lightheaded, and being touched by unseen hands while sitting in the cells. Or walk either the East or West Cellblock, where you might just hear some ghostly footsteps behind you. Some people have even had small rocks thrown at them from atop the cellblocks.

THE WEEPING WOMAN IN GRAY

If you ever find yourself at Camp Chase Confederate Cemetery in Columbus, Ohio, find the grave of Benjamin F. Allen and listen very closely. If you hear the faint sound of a woman weeping, you're in the presence of the cemetery's Lady in Gray.

THE HISTORY

Established in May 1861, Camp Chase served as a prison for Confederate officers during the Civil War. However, as the number of Confederate POWs grew, the prison could not be quite so selective. As 1863 dawned, Camp Chase held approximately 8,000 men of every rank.

The sheer number of prisoners soon overwhelmed Camp Chase. Men were forced to share bunks, and shortages of food, clothing, medicine, and other necessities were common. Under those conditions, the prisoners were vulnerable to disease and malnutrition, which led to many deaths—500 in one particular month alone, due to an outbreak of smallpox. Eventually, a cemetery was established at the camp to handle the large number of bodies.

Although Camp Chase was closed shortly after the war, the cemetery remains. Today, it contains the graves of more than 2,100 Confederate soldiers. Although restless spirits are commonly found where miserable deaths occurred, just one ghost is known to call Camp Chase its "home haunt": the famous Lady in Gray. Dressed in a flowing gray dress with a veil hiding her face, she is often seen standing and sobbing over Allen's grave. At other times, she can be found weeping at the grave of an unidentified soldier. Occasionally, she leaves flowers on the tombstones.

The Lady in Gray has also been spotted walking among the many gravestones in the cemetery; she's even been observed passing right through the locked cemetery gates. No one knows who she was in life, but some speculate that she was Allen's wife. However, her attention to the grave of the unknown soldier baffles researchers. One thing seems certain, though: As long as the Camp Chase Confederate Cemetery exists, the Lady in Gray will watch over it.

THE LOYAL KEEPER OF THE WHITE RIVER LIGHT

Are you dedicated enough to your job to perform your duties until the day you die? What about the day after?

LET THERE BE LIGHT

In the late 1850s, local mill owners and merchants became concerned about frequent shipwrecks occurring where the White River emptied into Lake Michigan near Whitehall, Michigan. The narrow river connected the lumber mills of White Lake (an area called "The Lumber Queen of the World") and the Great Lakes shipping channels. The state legislature responded by approving the construction of and funding for a lighthouse; however, the White River Light would not be built for another 12 years.

In 1872, a beacon light was set up at the area's South Pier, and shipping captain William Robinson was granted the position of light keeper. In 1875, the White River Light Station was built, and Robinson and his beloved wife, Sarah, moved into the keeper's residence, where they happily raised their 11 children. Robinson often said he was so happy there that he would stay until his dying day. That happiness was marred by Sarah's unexpected death in 1891. Robinson, who had expected to live with her at the lighthouse until his retirement, was inconsolable. Grief-stricken, he poured all of his attention into tending the lighthouse.

LIKE (GRAND)FATHER, LIKE (GRAND)SON

As Robinson grew older, the Lighthouse Board began to consider his replacement, finally awarding the post to his grandson (and assistant keeper), Captain William Bush, in 1915. Although the board expected Bush to immediately take over Robinson's duties, he kindly allowed his grandfather to continue as keeper and remain in the keeper's residence for several years.

In 1919, after 47 years of loyal service, the board demanded that Robinson vacate the premises, but he refused. The board allegedly met and agreed to take legal action against Robinson if he didn't leave, but they never got the chance. Two weeks later, on the day before the deadline, Robinson died in his sleep. Bush moved into the residence, and the board was satisfied with their new man. But Captain Robinson stayed on, apparently still refusing to budge.

THUMP, THUMP, TAP

The lighthouse was decommissioned in 1960 and was turned into a museum in 1970. Today, museum staff and visitors believe that Robinson still occupies the building and continues his duties as lighthouse keeper. Curator Karen McDonnell lives in the lighthouse and reports hearing footsteps on the circular staircase in the middle of the night. She attributes this to Robinson, rather than natural causes, because of the unmistakable sound of his walking cane on the stairs.

McDonnell believes Robinson may have also gotten his wish—to stay in the lighthouse with his wife—because Sarah seems to have returned to the lighthouse as well. She helps with dusting and light housework, leaving display cases cleaner than they were before. Museum visitors often talk about feeling warm and safe inside the building and feeling a sense of love and peace. One tourist felt the presence of a smitten young couple, sitting in one of the window nooks.

WE'LL LEAVE THE LIGHT ON FOR YOU

Visitors are welcome to explore the museum, which is open from June through October, and learn more about the shipping history of the Great Lakes. Perhaps you could even get a guided tour from the light's first and most loyal keeper—William Robinson, a man devoted to his wife and his job, who saw no reason why death should interfere with either.

THE FEISTY FENTON WRAITHS

The Fenton Hotel Tavern & Grille in Fenton, Michigan, no longer operates as an inn, but certain spectral guests seem unaware of that. As a result, the fine restaurant on the main floor of this historic building may be one of Michigan's most haunted places.

THE HISTORY

Built in 1856 and originally known as the Vermont House, the Fenton Hotel Tavern & Grille was bought and sold

several times before it received its current name.
Over the years, this remarkable building has been the
subject of numerous paranormal investigations and
séances, but the spooks that reside there seem
determined to avoid checking out.

The tin ceilings and original woodwork in the foyer and
dining area of the Fenton add to the illusion of a place
that's stuck in time. Maybe that's why Emery, the old hotel's
legendary janitor, still treads the creaky floorboards of
what used to be his room on the building's decrepit and
unused second floor. In life, Emery was a kindly gent who
was a bit of a workaholic. When the last customer leaves
in the evening, it is not uncommon for the staff to hear
Emery banging on the floor of his room as if to say,
"Get this place cleaned up!"

The hotel bar is another hot spot for unexplained
phenomena. Bartenders have seen wine glasses scoot right
off the stemware racks and fly across the room. Phantom
voices call the staff members by name, and unseen entities
brush up against them. Patrons once saw a mysterious
shadow figure hug a bartender—while the bartender
remained completely unaware of the affectionate display.

The Fenton's most unusual phenomenon—the thirsty ghost—
occurs from time to time at Table 32: It is there that a man
sits down and orders a shot of Jack Daniel's on the rocks,
but before the wait staff can get the drink to the table,
the man vanishes.

Table 32 is not the only haunted dining spot at the Fenton.
A waitress and a manager have both seen a top-hat-clad

shadow figure lounging at Table 63; this entity has even been captured in photos. The dining room is also rumored to house one overly frisky ghost that some waitresses claim has pinched their backsides.

THE FENTON'S FEMME FATALES

Not all of the ghosts at the Fenton Hotel Tavern & Grille are male; supposedly, the spirits of some "working girls" who once lived on the third floor also remain. According to one legend, a young prostitute hung herself in the downstairs restroom and still makes her presence known there by opening and closing stall doors; another version says that the ghostly girl was an unwed, pregnant traveler. Regardless of who she was in life, strange things do happen in the ladies room. Once, a customer seated in a stall watched in disbelief as an unseen force lifted a strand of her long hair and then dropped it back into place. Another time, a workman, who had been sent in to complete some repairs, was unable to open an unlocked stall. After he felt a vaporous mist float through him, he was finally able to open the door. Perhaps this spirit was a modest ghost that just needed some privacy.

THE SEAL OF DISAPPROVAL

The second-floor hotel rooms are off-limits to customers, but in the mid-2000s, *Weird Michigan* author Linda Godfrey was given an evening tour of the area. That night, she heard loud, unintelligible whispering directly in her ear while she, a hostess, and another researcher stood quietly in the hallway. Later in the investigation, Godfrey discovered that the viewfinder on her camera was covered with fresh candle wax—however, she had not been near a lit candle all evening. Godfrey felt as though some unseen entity was literally attempting to block her view of that section of the hotel. Perhaps, like all hotel guests, the ghosts of the Fenton simply value their privacy.

In February 1904, the Fenton Hotel's second- and third-story front porches were dragged away by a team of frightened horses. When something at the railroad depot spooked the equines, they took off galloping through town and thundered past the hotel, pulling down support posts as they went. Amazingly, no one was hurt, but the porches were never rebuilt.

THE HAUNTING OF THE HOLLY HOTEL

The Holly Hotel in Holly, Michigan, is more than just a historical landmark—it's allegedly a hotbed of paranormal activity. But are the stories surrounding the place fact or fiction?

A HOTEL WITH A FUTURE

In the 1860s, America's railway systems were enjoying epic expansion. As tracks were laid, more people and more products than ever before were crisscrossing the nation. Major midwestern cities such as Detroit and Chicago were bustling, and the need for hotels near stations was growing because they served locals and travelers alike.

Built in 1863, the Holly Hotel (originally called the Hirst Hotel after its first proprietor, John Hirst) and the surrounding area certainly looked different in that era than they do today. Back then, the building was larger than it is now, and Martha Street—on which the Holly stands— was lined with taverns that hosted brawls so often that it was dubbed "Battle Alley" (a nickname that persists to this day). It might've been rough-and-tumble outside the hotel, but inside, the Holly boasted hot water, elegant rooms, fine dining, and a large staff, which set a tone for luxury that continues to this day, even though the establishment is only a restaurant now.

In 1912, Hirst sold the hotel to Joseph P. Allen, who renamed it the Holly Inn. But in 1913, a massive fire completely destroyed the building's second and third floors. Hirst, once a cigar-smoking, boisterous host, was crushed by the loss of the beautiful hotel that he'd built; when he passed away seven years later, the townspeople said that he never overcame the grief that he suffered following the devastating fire. Enter the Holly Hotel's first ghost.

Employees have long said that John Hirst haunts the Holly. The smell of cigar smoke is often perceived at the bar, even when no one is smoking. And over the years, numerous visitors have spotted the figure of a man wearing a frock coat and a top hat, and disembodied laughter is frequently heard traveling from the stairs down to what was once the hotel's lower-level parlor.

A FIERY DÉJÀ VU AND MORE GHOSTLY FIGURES

Even if you don't believe in spooks, it's hard not to be freaked out by the fact that in 1978—exactly 65 years to the day *and hour* of the first disastrous fire—the Holly Hotel burned again. Although no one was killed, the fire caused more than a half million dollars of damage. The building was repaired, and once again, stories about ghosts roaming the halls came pouring in.

The spirit of Nora Kane—a frequent visitor to the hotel in her days among the living—still lingers at the Holly. When photographers are contracted to shoot weddings at the restaurant—a popular place for receptions due to its lush Victorian decor and fine food—they're warned that apparitions or strange shadows may obscure some of their photos. On the websites of paranormal investigators who have visited the Holly, wispy, cloudlike strands can be seen in images of the stairwell. Is it a trick of photography, or is Nora Kane walking into the shot? Guests and employees have also claimed to hear her singing near the piano when things get too quiet.

One of the most active spirits at the Holly Hotel is that of a fiery red-haired girl who likes to play with a meat cleaver in the kitchen. Disembodied giggles and footsteps have been reported there, and during a séance in the 1990s, the girl allegedly manifested. It is believed that, in life, she was either the daughter of Nora Kane or a young girl who died tragically after sustaining injuries at the livery stable that once stood adjacent to the hotel.

Other unexplainable phenomena at the hotel include sudden drops in temperature, floating orbs, phantom barking and the sound of a dog running down the halls, and appearances of a Native American figure that vanishes as quickly as it arrives.

NOT JUST A GHOST MOTEL

The legacy of the Holly Hotel is worth studying, regardless of potential spirit activity, and the proprietors tend to focus on promoting it as a historical landmark and fine-dining establishment. High tea is held there weekly, and the grounds are often used for private events.

But for those who believe in ghosts, it remains a popular destination. Often cited as one of the most haunted places in America, the Holly Hotel may hold secrets that none of us can unlock—at least not on this plane of existence.

BEER, WINE, AND SPIRITS: THE HAUNTED LEMP MANSION

There is no other place in St. Louis, Missouri, with a ghostly history quite like the Lemp Mansion. It has served as many things over the years—stately home, boarding house, restaurant, bed-and-breakfast—but it has never lost the notoriety of being the most haunted place in the city. In fact, in 1980, Life magazine called the Lemp Mansion "one of the ten most haunted places in America."

The Lemp brewery, and the Lemp family itself, gained recognition during the mid-1800s. Although they were credited with making one of the first lager beers in the United States and once rivaled the annual sales of Anheuser–Busch, few people remember much about the Lemps today—most people in St. Louis can barely even recall that the Lemps once made beer. They are now more familiar with the family's mansion on the city's south side than with the decaying brewery that stands two blocks away. The Lemps have been gone for years, but their old house stands as a reminder of their wealth and the tragedies that plagued them. Perhaps that's why there's still an aura of sadness looming over the place.

During the day, the house is a bustling restaurant, filled with people and activity, but at night, many people believe the old mansion is haunted. Are its ghosts the restless spirits of the Lemps wandering the corridors of their former home? It seems possible, given the enormous number of tragedies that struck the family.

THE LEMP EMPIRE BEGINS

Adam Lemp left Germany in 1836, and by 1838 had settled in St. Louis. He had learned the brewer's trade as a young man, and he soon introduced the city to one of the first American lagers, a crisp, clean beer that required months of storage in a cool, dark place to obtain its unique flavor. This new beer quickly became a regional favorite.

Business prospered, and by the 1850s, thanks to the demand for lager, Lemp's Western Brewing Company was one of the largest in the city. When Adam Lemp died in

1862, his son William took the reins, and the company entered its period of greatest prominence.

After the death of his father, William began a major expansion of the brewery. He purchased more land and constructed a new brewery—the largest in St. Louis. In 1899, the Lemps introduced their famous Falstaff beer, which became a favorite across the country. Lemp was the first brewery to establish coast-to-coast distribution of its beer, and the company grew so large that as many as 100 horses were needed to pull the delivery wagons in St. Louis alone.

In 1876, during the time of his company's greatest success, William purchased a home for his family a short distance away from the brewery. He immediately began renovating and expanding the house, which had been built in the early 1860s, decorating it with original artwork, hand-carved wood decor, and ornately painted ceilings. The mansion featured a tunnel that traveled from the basement of the house along a quarried shaft and exited at the brewery. Ironically, it was in the midst of all this success that the Lemp family's troubles began.

DEATH COMES CALLING

The first death in the family was that of Frederick Lemp, William's favorite son and heir to the Lemp empire. As the most ambitious and hardworking of the Lemp children, he'd been groomed to take over the family business. He was well liked and happily married but spent countless hours at the brewery working to improve the company's future. In 1901, his health began to fail, and, in December of that year, he died at age 28. Many believe that he worked himself to death.

Frederick's death devastated his parents, especially his father. William's friends and coworkers said he was never the same afterward. He was rarely seen in public and walked to the brewery using the tunnel beneath the house.

On January 1, 1904, William suffered another crushing blow with the death of his closest friend, fellow brewer Frederick Pabst. This tragedy left William nervous and unsettled, and his physical and mental health began to deteriorate. On February 13, 1904, his suffering became unbearable. After breakfast, he went upstairs to his bedroom and shot himself with a revolver. No suicide note was ever found.

In November 1904, William, Jr., became president of the William J. Lemp Brewing Company. With his inheritance, he filled the house with servants, built country houses, and spent huge sums on carriages, clothing, and art.

Will's wife, Lillian, nicknamed the "Lavender Lady" because of her fondness for that color, was soon spending the Lemp fortune as quickly as her husband. They eventually divorced in 1906, causing a scandal throughout St. Louis. When it was all over, the Lavender Lady went into seclusion.

LESS DRINKING, MORE DEATH

In 1919, the 18th Amendment was passed, prohibiting the manufacture, transportation, and sale of alcohol in the United States. This signaled the end for many brewers, including the Lemps. Many hoped that Congress would repeal the amendment, but Will decided not to wait. He closed down the plant without notice, thus closing the door on the Lemp empire.

Will sold the famous Lemp "Falstaff" logo to brewer Joseph Griesedieck for $25,000. In 1922, he sold the brewery to the International Shoe Co. for a fraction of its estimated worth ($7 million before Prohibition).

With Prohibition destroying the brewery, the 1920s looked to be a dismal decade for the Lemp family. And it began on a tragic note, with the suicide of Elsa Lemp Wright in 1920. The second member of the family to commit suicide, Elsa was the wealthiest woman in St. Louis after inheriting her share of her father's estate. After a stormy marriage to wealthy industrialist Thomas Wright between 1910 and 1918, the couple divorced but then remarried in March 1920. Shortly after, Elsa inexplicably shot herself. No letter was ever found.

Will and his brother Edwin rushed to Elsa's house when they heard of their sister's suicide. Will had only one comment: "That's the Lemp family for you." Will's own death came a short time later. While sitting in his office in the mansion, Will shot himself in the chest. His secretary found him lying in a pool of blood, and he died before a doctor could be summoned. As with his father and sister before him, Will had left no indication as to why he had ended his life.

Oddly, Will seemed to have had no intention of killing himself. After the sale of the brewery, he had discussed selling off the rest of his assets and said he wanted to rest and travel. He and his second wife were even planning a trip to Europe. Friends were baffled by his sudden death.

With William, Jr., gone and his brothers, Charles and Edwin, involved with their own endeavors, it seemed that the days of the Lemp empire had come to an end. But the days of Lemp tragedy were not yet over.

Charles was never very involved with the Lemp Brewery. His work had mostly been in the banking and financial industries, and he sometimes dabbled in politics as well. In the 1920s, Charles moved back into the Lemp Mansion.

Charles was a mysterious figure who became odd and reclusive with age. A lifelong bachelor, he lived alone in the rambling old house, and by age 77, he was arthritic and ill. He had grown quite eccentric and developed a morbid attachment to the Lemp family home. Because of the history of the place, his brother Edwin often encouraged Charles to move out, but he refused. Finally, when he could stand it no more, he became the fourth member of the Lemp family to take his own life.

On May 10, 1949, one of the staff members found Charles dead in his second-floor bedroom. He had shot himself at some point during the night. He was the only member of the family to leave a suicide note behind. He wrote: "In case I am found dead, blame it on no one but me."

The Lemp family, once so large and prosperous, had been nearly destroyed in less than a century. Only Edwin Lemp remained, and he had long avoided the life that had turned so tragic for the rest of his family. He was known as a quiet, reclusive man who lived a peaceful life on his secluded estate. In 1970, Edwin, the last of the Lemps, passed away quietly of natural causes at age 90.

LEMP MANSION HAUNTINGS

After the death of Charles Lemp, the grand family mansion was sold and turned into a boarding house. It soon fell on hard times and began to deteriorate along with the neighborhood. In later years, stories emerged that residents of the boarding house often complained of ghostly knocks and phantom footsteps inside. As these tales spread, it became increasingly hard to find tenants to occupy the rooms, so the old Lemp Mansion was rarely filled.

The decline of the house continued until 1975, when Dick Pointer and his family purchased it. The Pointers began remodeling and renovating the place, working for years to turn it into a restaurant and inn. But the Pointers soon realized they were not alone in the house. Workers told of ghostly events occurring, such as strange sounds, tools that vanished and appeared again in other places, and an overwhelming feeling that they were being watched.

After the restaurant opened, staff members began to report their own odd experiences. Glasses were seen lifting off the bar and flying through the air, inexplicable sounds were heard, and some people even glimpsed actual apparitions. Visitors to the house reported that doors locked and unlocked on their own, voices and sounds came from nowhere, and even the Lavender Lady was spotted on occasion.

These strange events continue today, so it is no surprise that the inn attracts ghost hunters from around the country. Many spend the night in the house and report their own bizarre happenings, from eerie sounds to strange photographs. One woman awoke to see the specter of a lady standing next to her bed. The ghost raised a finger to her lips, as if asking the woman not to scream, and then vanished.

Paul Pointer manages the business today, along with his sisters, Mary and Patty. They all accept the ghosts as part of the ambience of the historic old home. As Paul once said, "People come here expecting to experience weird things, and fortunately for us, they are rarely disappointed."

THE MAUDLIN SPIRITS OF THE MOUNDS THEATRE

In 1922, the Mounds Theatre opened on the east side of St. Paul, Minnesota, to showcase silent films. A few dramatic characters from that era are said to remain in the restored Art Deco building, but these entities are not confined to the silver screen.

AN EERIE FIND

The most frightening spook at the Mounds is the spectral male figure that lurks in the dusty, antiquated projection room. Building director Raeann Ruth and three paranormal investigators who spent a night in the room all

reported hearing a male voice alternately cry and swear up a storm. They also witnessed an angry male ghost staring at them with dark, sunken eyes. It certainly didn't help to alleviate any fears when the group discovered an antique Ouija board lying amid the old projection equipment.

TRAGEDIES SPAWN TERRORS

A more benign ghost is dressed as an usher and seems to be crying. According to legend, he was a theater worker who found his beloved cuddling with someone else. It is believed that after death, he stayed attached to the scene of his life's greatest tragedy.

Tragic may also be the best way to describe another Mounds Theatre ghost—a young girl who skips around the stage bouncing a ball. During a recent renovation (2001–2003), a small dress and a child's shoe were found hidden in the theater. Some believe that these items could be linked to a possible child assault, which could explain why the girl's spirit still roams the theater.

NEW LIFE FOR OLD SPIRITS

A nonprofit children's theater troupe now owns the building, thanks to the generosity of former owner George Hardenbergh, who bequeathed it to the group, Portage for Youth, in 2001, rather than see the grand old place demolished. Perhaps the influence of these happy young people will eventually banish the sad spirits lingering at the theater and help restore its original festive air.

GRIGGS MANSION

A notoriously haunted house in St. Paul, Minnesota, changes hands, and then all paranormal activity ceases. Was the house ever haunted? If so, what made the once-frisky ghosts decide to pack up and leave? It's a question that is difficult to answer. A house that's haunted to some seems completely benign to others. Who is right? Let's examine the evidence.

FIRST FRIGHTS

Built in 1883 by wholesale grocery tycoon Chauncey W. Griggs, the imposing 24-room Griggs Mansion features high ceilings, a dark interior, and a stone facade that looks decidedly menacing. Although the home bears his name, Griggs lived there for only a scant four years before moving to sunnier climes on the West Coast. After that, the house changed hands quite frequently, which some say is a sure sign that the place was haunted.

The first ghost sightings at the house date back to 1915, when a young maid—who was despondent over a breakup—hanged herself on the mansion's fourth floor. Soon after the woman's burial, her spirit was allegedly seen roaming the building's hallways. According to witnesses, the ghost of Charles Wade arrived next. In life, he was the mansion's gardener and caretaker; in death, he reportedly liked to cruise the building's library.

UNEXPLAINED ACTIVITY

Strange occurrences are the norm at the Griggs Mansion. Over the years, residents have reported hearing disembodied footsteps traveling up and down the staircases, seeing doors open and close by themselves, hearing voices coming from unoccupied rooms, and experiencing all manner of unexplainable incidents, which suggest that the Griggs Mansion is indeed haunted.

In 1939, the mansion was donated to the St. Paul Gallery and School of Art. During the 1950s, staffer Dr. Delmar Rolb claimed that he saw the apparition of a "tall thin man" in his apartment in the basement of the building. In 1964, Carl L. Weschcke—a publisher of books relating to the occult—acquired the house. He said that as soon as he would close a particular window, it would mysteriously reopen. Determined to stop this game, Weschcke nailed the window shut; however, when he returned home the next day, it was open once again.

GHOSTBUSTERS

In 1969, reporters from a local newspaper spent a night at the Griggs Mansion. The journalists—who were all initially skeptics—became believers after spending a harrowing night on the premises; unexplained footsteps and an unnerving feeling that a presence accompanied them were enough to do the trick. The frightened reporters fled the mansion in the wee hours of the morning and never returned.

MORE SKEPTICS

In 1982, Tibor and Olga Zoltai purchased the mansion. "When we first moved in, there were people who would cross to the other side of the street to pass the house," Olga recalled in an interview with a local newspaper. "One even threw a piece of Christ's cross into the yard." However, in nearly three decades of living inside the reputedly haunted house, the couple has never experienced anything out of the ordinary. To show just how silly they found the ghost stories, the playful couple assembled an "emergency kit" that contained a clove of garlic, a bottle of holy water, a crucifix, and a stake. They figured that these items would provide ample protection against any restless spirits in the house.

YEA OR NAY

So are there ghosts at the Griggs Mansion or not? Those who claim to have witnessed paranormal activity there stand firmly behind their stories; those who have not offer other possible explanations. "If you go into a situation thinking something is going to happen, it probably will," reasons Chad Lewis, author of *Haunted St. Paul*, in reference to the terrifying night that the reporters spent at the mansion. That said, however, Lewis isn't convinced that the ghost stories surrounding the Griggs Mansion are mere figments of people's imaginations. "I think the stories are true. I don't think people are making them up or hallucinating or suffering from mental illness. I think something happened there, but what happened there, I don't know."

GHOSTS OF GLENSHEEN

In 1905, self-made millionaire Chester Congdon was one of Minnesota's richest men. When the banking and iron-mining magnate and his wife, Clara, moved into their stupendous mansion on the shore of Lake Superior in 1908, they never dreamed that their elegant home would someday be famous for murder...and ghosts.

The Congdons named their sprawling estate "Glensheen." The brick lakefront house features multiple gables and chimneys and 39 richly furnished rooms. The Congdons spared no expense on their state-of-the-art abode, equipping it with electricity, running water, and a humidification system and covering the grounds with lush gardens where they entertained Minnesota's elite with impressive parties.

Chester only lived in his dream home for eight years: He died in 1916 at age 63. The estate passed to Clara and then to the couple's youngest daughter, Elisabeth. To this day, the house retains most of the family's original furnishings, which makes the area where a grisly double murder took place seem even eerier to visitors.

FAMILY TIES, LIES, AND SIGHS

In 1977, Elisabeth was 83 years old and was partially paralyzed. She had never married, although she had adopted two girls: Jennifer—who married a businessman and led a quiet life in Racine, Wisconsin—and Marjorie, the black sheep of the family. Elisabeth's life of luxury ended violently when an intruder smothered the helpless woman in her sleep with her own pink satin pillow; he also bludgeoned Elisabeth's protective night nurse, Velma Pietila, with a candlestick.

Suspicion immediately fell on Marjorie, but it was her husband, Roger Caldwell, who was charged with killing the elderly heiress to obtain Marjorie's $8 million share of the estate; Marjorie was charged with aiding and abetting him in the crime. Caldwell went to prison and later confessed to the crime, but Marjorie was acquitted. In fact, the trial's jurors felt so sorry for her that they threw her a posttrial party!

That was a nice gesture, but even being honored so highly was not enough to change Marjorie's basic nature. Although she did get her hands on a pile of her dead mother's money, her life deteriorated further thereafter. In 1981, she married Wallace Hagen (without divorcing Roger Caldwell), and in 1984, she was convicted of arson and insurance fraud in Minnesota. By 1992, Marjorie and

Hagen, were living in Arizona, where she was again found guilty of arson. After her conviction but before she went to jail, Hagen died of a mysterious drug overdose. Marjorie was arrested and charged with his murder, but the charges were later dropped. Marjorie was released from prison in 2004, but in 2007, she was arrested again—this time on charges of committing fraud and forgery. In 2010, she again made headlines when she tried to get her probation dropped so that she could move into an assisted-living facility in Arizona.

A SOFT SHEEN OF SPIRITS

Meanwhile, Glensheen remains as grand as ever. Now owned by the University of Minnesota-Duluth, the mansion is used for art fairs and theatrical productions, including readings of the macabre stories of Edgar Allen Poe during Halloween season. The house and gardens are also open for public tours. And although its tour guides are reportedly tight-lipped about hauntings, it is believed that the spirits of Elisabeth and Velma have never left the place. People have seen misty figures floating about, heard unidentifiable noises, and felt cold chills when viewing the room in which Elisabeth died.

In one story that was recounted in *The Minnesota Road Guide to Haunted Locations,* an employee felt something pulling on his ankles while he was standing on a ladder. Thinking that a coworker had snuck up the ladder to play a prank, he turned to face the culprit, but no one was there— at least, no one that he could see.

Who could blame Elisabeth and Velma for lingering at the Glensheen Mansion? It's certainly a beautiful place to spend eternity. Five years before Elisabeth Congdon was killed, Patty Duke starred in a dark thriller filmed at Glensheen. The movie's title? *You'll Like My Mother.*

THE "GRAY LADY" OF EVANSVILLE, INDIANA

The Willard Library in Evansville, Indiana, has a long history of supernatural activity. But while multiple ghosts typically inhabit many haunted buildings, only one spirit seems to peruse the stacks at this old Victorian library— an entity known as the Lady in Gray.

NOT SHY AT ALL

According to local reports, the Lady in Gray has been haunting the Willard Library since at least the 1930s. The first known encounter with her occurred in 1937, when a janitor ran into the lonely ghost as he entered the library's cellar to stoke its furnace. There, he saw a mysterious woman dressed all in gray. A veil was draped from her face to her shoes, and she glowed ethereally in the darkness.

That may have been the first confirmed encounter with the Gray Lady, but it certainly wasn't the last. In fact, according to library employees and patrons, this spirit seems to go out of its way to make its presence known. On one occasion, the members of a local genealogy group noticed the distinct scent of perfume in the library's research room.

None of the group members was wearing perfume at the time, and no one else had entered the room while they were there.

Margaret Maier, who worked at the library for more than four decades, also smelled the Gray Lady's musky perfume at her own home. Maier speculated that the spirit briefly followed her home while the children's room of the library was undergoing renovations. In addition to the scent of perfume, Maier and her sister reported feeling an unseen presence in their midst, as well as an inexplicable chill at Maier's home.

SPOOKY SHENANIGANS

She clearly means no harm, but the Lady in Gray isn't above playing pranks on library staffers. One night, Bettye Elaine Miller, who was head librarian from 1972 to 1975, was working late when she heard water running on the second floor. She rushed upstairs to find that a bathroom faucet had been mysteriously turned on. Later, another librarian using the same bathroom watched in horror as a faucet turned on by itself.

Over the years, reports of paranormal activity at the Willard Library have become so commonplace that, with the library's permission, the *Evansville Courier & Press* installed three internet-connected "ghost cams" in the building so that curious ghost hunters can try to catch a glimpse of the Gray Lady. The cameras have proven quite popular with fans of the paranormal, logging hundreds of thousands of hits since they first went online. Want to check it out for yourself? Visit WillardGhost.com.

A GHOST REVEALED

Of course, everyone wants to know the identity of the mysterious Gray Lady. Local historians believe that she is the ghost of Louise Carpenter, the daughter of Willard Carpenter, who funded the construction of the library and for whom it was named. According to reports, Louise was greatly displeased with the fact that when her father died, he left a great deal of his money for the construction of a public library. She even tried to sue the library's board of trustees, claiming that her father was "of unsound mind and…unduly influenced in establishing the library."

Louise's lawsuit was unsuccessful, and she was unable to stop the library's construction. A theory among many ghost hunters suggests that, upon her death in 1908, Louise's spirit came to reside within the library and will stay there until the property is returned to the Carpenter family, which is quite unlikely.

Libraries are popular haunts for ghosts, but few have logged as many reputable sightings and paranormal occurrences as the Willard Library. It very well may be the most haunted library in the United States, thanks to a gray-clad spirit that still holds a grudge, even from beyond the grave.

THE GHOST OF THE GIPPER

The University of Notre Dame is rife with history and tradition. Founded in 1842 in South Bend, Indiana, this school is known for its academics—and football. And while the team is busy "winning one for the Gipper," the Gipper himself is busy haunting his old campus.

WHO IS THE GIPPER?

The Gipper, of course, was Notre Dame football legend George Gipp. As the school's first All-American, Gipp played a variety of positions—all very well. But like many young men, Gipp also enjoyed a good party and a bit of gambling. Some say that after a night of such revelry, Gipp returned to his dorm—Washington Hall—after curfew and found himself locked out. This was in December 1920, and with no way to call for help, Gipp curled up on the steps and fell asleep. Many believe that this night spent in the elements is what caused Gipp to come down with the dreaded duo of strep throat and pneumonia. Because antibiotics were not yet available, Gipp's condition soon became grave.

On his deathbed, Gipp reportedly had a heartfelt conversation with his coach, Knute Rockne. He told Rockne that someday, when the coach needed to rally his team to victory, he should mention his name and ask that team to go out there and "win one for the Gipper." And in an inspirational and oft-repeated speech to his squad a few years later, Rockne did just that.

Maybe Gipp has been hanging around in case he is needed to help his beloved Fighting Irish on the gridiron, or maybe he is just having a little fun. Whatever the case, before Washington Hall was converted into classrooms in the 1950s, phantom footsteps and doors slamming of their own accord were usually attributed to the ghost of Gipp. Now that the facility houses the theater department, Gipp is thought to haunt the stage and other rooms nearby. Drama students working late at night have heard strange music and other noises in the building. And many students have reported feeling that someone is standing beside them just as they get a fleeting glimpse of a ghost.

THE GHOSTS OF WISCONSIN'S BLACK POINT MANSION

Like many spectral beings, some ghost stories evaporate like misty ectoplasm when studied closely. In other words, they don't hold up to scrutiny when examined thoroughly. But the ghosts of the Black Point Mansion on Wisconsin's Geneva Lake boast a solid history to back up the spooky legend of their origin.

WHAT HAPPENED AT BLACK POINT?

In 1888, wealthy Chicagoan Conrad Seipp built a 20-room summer home on the southern shore of Geneva Lake. Known as Black Point Mansion, Seipp's vacation house looks much the same today as it did back then, with an imposing four-story tower that rises above the black oak trees for which it was named. But according to local legend, on stormy nights, the cupola at the tower's peak holds the restless spirits of a priest and nuns who drowned in the lake many years ago.

Unlike many urban legends, this tale has elements of truth to it: On July 7, 1895, Father James Hogan, a beloved Catholic priest from Harvard, Illinois, did indeed drown in Geneva Lake within sight of Black Point Mansion. But the others who died were not Catholic sisters but rather Father Hogan's *actual* sister Mary; his brother Dr. John Hogan; the doctor's wife, Kittie; their two-year-old child; and a steamboat captain.

On that fateful day, the Hogan family had taken a train from Illinois to Williams Bay on the northwestern shore of Geneva Lake. From there, they boarded a small steamboat to visit friends who lived nearby. As the day wore on, storm clouds began to gather, so the family decided to make a fast retreat before the weather worsened. Eyeing the darkening sky, the captain of the steamer *Dispatch* advised the group to postpone their trip until after the storm had passed. But the Hogans persuaded him to make the trip anyway, and the *Dispatch* began what would be its final crossing of Geneva Lake.

The anxious passengers were more than halfway through their journey when a squall kicked up. The storm quickly turned so violent that the small vessel could not make it to the nearest landing—a park near Black Point Mansion. The captain blew his distress whistle over and over, but no one could get to the steamer before it capsized, tossing all five passengers and the captain into the deep spring-fed lake. The mansion's tower may well have been the last thing any of them saw before succumbing to the cold, dark water.

Anguished witnesses on shore saw the baby's white dress fluttering in the harsh wind...and then the family was gone. It took some time to recover the bodies, but newspapers said that the doctor was found on the lake bottom with his hands in an attitude of prayer; Mary still wore her ladylike gloves and held her purse; and Father Hogan was lying as if merely at rest. Seventy-five priests and a large crowd of parishioners attended his funeral.

A LAKE MONSTER'S BALL

Black Point Mansion's haunted tower is not the area's only supernatural claim to fame. Before European settlers came to Geneva Lake, the Potawatomi people who lived there believed that fierce water spirits fought with thunderbirds in the lake to cause the kind of sudden storm that sank the *Dispatch*. They also thought that the lake was home to an eel-like monster that would pull down canoes during bad weather. And in the mid-to-late 1800s, numerous residents and tourists claimed to have seen a giant creature—which they dubbed Jenny—swimming along the lakeshore.

One of the people who spotted Jenny was a minister from nearby Delavan. And in July 1892—just three years before the drowning of the Hogan family—the *Chicago Tribune* reported that three fishermen saw a 100-foot-long monster in the lake. The sighting occurred in front of the very park that the captain of the *Dispatch* was trying to reach when the steamer went down.

TAKE AN EXCURSION ON THE LAKE...
IF YOU DARE

Today, Black Point Mansion is owned by the state of Wisconsin; it serves as a museum, and despite the fact that it retains nearly all of its original furniture, the building itself is not believed to harbor any ghosts—just the open cupola. From May through October, tourists can still venture out on the lake by steamboat to get exactly the same view of the mansion and its tower that the ill-fated Hogan family had on that tragic day in 1895.

THE SISTERS OF KEMPER HALL

Kemper Hall—which is situated on the shore of Lake Michigan in Kenosha, Wisconsin—is one of the Dairy State's oldest buildings. The structure originally served as the home of Wisconsin's first congressman, Charles Durkee. When he became governor of the Utah Territory in 1865, Durkee donated the estate to the Kenosha Female Seminary. In 1878, the Sisters of Saint Mary took over the property, renamed it Kemper Hall, and turned it into a preparatory school for girls—and that's when many of its ghostly stories began.

THE SPECTRAL SISTER SUPERIOR

Perhaps the most famous of the ghost stories involving Kemper Hall revolves around Sister Margaret Clare, the school's first Sister Superior and the embodiment of the stereotypical stern parochial-school nun. Sister Margaret Clare was well liked in her order, but students knew her for her demanding nature and unrelenting temper. One legend says that the nun met her end when an angry student pushed her down the spiral staircase that led to the school's observatory; other rumors suggest that she fell down the stairs after tripping on her own habit. Not surprisingly, the observatory and staircase still attract visitors. Many who have peered down the stairwell at night claim that they have glimpsed her shattered body staring back at them from the bottom. The problem with these tales is that Sister Margaret Clare actually died of natural causes in 1921. Still, the reports of the fallen nun persist; perhaps it's a different nun.

A MYSTERIOUS DISAPPEARANCE

Sister Margaret Clare may have gone to her grave harboring a sinister secret about the mysterious disappearance of another nun: Sister Augusta. In 1899, Sister Augusta arrived at Kemper Hall for an annual retreat; but shortly thereafter—on January 2, 1900—she vanished without a trace. Some said that she'd been driven to the edge of madness by the amount of work she'd been given and was granted a time-off request. But her disappearance seemed suspect to authorities, who undertook a search that stretched all the way back to Sister Augusta's hometown of St. Louis, Missouri. Then, on January 5, Kemper Hall sent word to the nun's family and the authorities that Sister Augusta had been found, safe and sound, in Springfield, Missouri. However, the school failed to offer an explanation for why she had left behind her handbag, her crucifix, and her insignia of the holy Sisterhood. Just three days later, Sister Augusta's body washed up on the shore of Lake Michigan. Her death was ruled a suicide, and to this day, locals still report seeing a spectral nun in tears walking along the beach. Many maintenance workers and watchmen have also reported hearing a woman sobbing in Kemper Hall late at night, but when they investigate, they find no one. Sister Augusta may well be the crying nun that so many hear, but she does not cry alone.

PICTURE OF THE PARANORMAL

Kemper Center, Inc., has not allowed paranormal investigators to access Kemper Hall since it took control of the building shortly after the school closed in 1975. But much of the property is now a public park, and on several occasions, nighttime visitors have seen a nun—perhaps Sister Augusta or Sister Margaret Clare—peering at them from the windows of the former school. People visiting Kemper Hall for wedding receptions have also reported hearing crying and footsteps in hallways that are clearly unoccupied by the living.

In 1997, a television crew from WTMJ in Milwaukee filmed a story at the original Durkee Mansion. The shoot went off without issue, but when the crew was editing the footage, they found that the picture turned to static every time a portrait of Charles Durkee entered the frame. It seems that the Sisters of Kemper Hall have maintained an ethereal presence in the building, but perhaps they're not the only spirits who still consider the place home.

FOND DU LAC GHOSTS HAUNT THEIR OLD STOMPING GROUNDS

Listed on the National Register of Historic places, the Ramada Plaza Hotel in Fond du Lac, Wisconsin, is also on more than one "most haunted" list. Built in the 1920s, this structure was originally known as the Hotel Retlaw, after owner Walter Schroeder. ("Retlaw" is "Walter" spelled backward.) And even though Walter is no longer alive, he appears to have remained at his namesake hotel.

THE HISTORY

In its heyday, this eight-story building was one of the premier hotels in Wisconsin along with several others that were owned by Schroeder. Located at the junction of four major Wisconsin highways, the inn attracted some prominent guests, such as John F. Kennedy, Eleanor Roosevelt, Hubert Humphrey, and numerous Wisconsin politicians.

Over the years, there have been so many stories of ghosts at the hotel that employees started keeping a log to record the activity. Some say that Walter Schroeder was murdered there and that it's his ghost that haunts the property. But it seems that he's not alone. The most haunted area of the hotel is Room 717, where visitors and staff have heard screams and other noises—all while the room is empty. Faucets and lights turn themselves on and off, and the TV changes stations on its own—this ghost seems to favor C-SPAN.

Other paranormal activity has been observed throughout the hotel. Strange humming when no one is around, a ghostly figure walking into walls, and an odd glow in the banquet room are all part of the fun. One frequently seen apparition is a redheaded woman in a white bathrobe; she disappears into the wall when startled.

In addition, the chandelier in the ballroom sometimes sways for no reason, and an employee spotted a couple dancing there. He thought it was rather sweet...until the pair vanished before his eyes.

On a side note, it was believed that the ghost of Walter Schroeder also haunted the Retlaw Theater, which was located just a block away from the hotel. Coincidence? Probably not.

WALKER HOUSE: KEEPING THE MINER SPIRIT ALIVE

Mineral Point, Wisconsin, was a prime lead-mining town in the early 19th century. The mineral-rich bluffs attracted miners to the area, and a railroad line that ended there made the southern part of town the perfect place to build an inn. Established in 1836, the Walker House served many visitors over the years. Some lived there while they worked the mines; many were just passing through; and a few others decided to stay...forever.

IN THE BEGINNING

After the Walker House opened, it quickly gained a reputation as an upscale inn. The first floor featured a pub, a kitchen, and a large area that was used for food storage; the second floor included two rooms that offered fine dining; and the third floor consisted of guest rooms for the many miners, gamblers, travelers, and railroad workers who decided to stop in for a bit of shut-eye.

The inn was open for more than a century before it closed its doors in 1957. Since then, the building has been in a state of flux, and it has been placed on the market several times. Numerous pubs and inns have occupied the space, but they never seemed to flourish. At the start of the 21st century, the building was listed as one of the ten most endangered historical structures in Wisconsin. Then, in 2005, it was brought back to life as an inn, complete with a restaurant, a pub, and, naturally, a few ghosts. But the building's new life would be short lived: As of this writing, the Walker House is once again closed and for sale.

A HAUNTINGLY GOOD TIME

The most famous spirit at the Walker House is that of William Caffee, who was hanged on the premises in November 1842. Caffee apparently got into an argument with another man and shot him. While the shooting may have been self-defense or even an accident, Caffee's trial was quick—and, some say, rigged—and he was sentenced to a public hanging. More than 4,000 people turned out to watch the spectacle, which included the condemned man riding to the gallows in his own coffin. With two beer bottles in hand, he played a funeral dirge on the sides of the casket. Apparently, he had a good sense of humor—even at the end.

Although Caffee was not able to prevent his own death, no one can force him to leave the Walker House, as his spirit has remained there for more than 150 years. His specter has been seen walking the halls, and he may be responsible for doorknobs mysteriously turning on their own on the second floor. Staff members and guests both say that they have experienced his pranks; he especially likes to pull employees' hair. In 1981, the inn's owner watched Caffee's headless ghost sit on a bench on the back porch for quite some time. A few weeks later, another employee saw Caffee—with his head intact—walking down the hallway on the second floor. Both times, Caffee was dressed in a rumpled gray outfit that was typical of miners of his day.

While he is certainly the building's most prolific ghost, Caffee doesn't seem to be the only spirit hanging out at the Walker House; in fact, one psychic claimed that 22 ghosts were on the property. One was quite devoted to the most recent owners and would tell anyone who filled in for them to "Get out of here! You're not the owner." Employees have seen an apparition watching from the top of the staircase, clearly not happy with how things are run. Many think that it is the spirit of a past owner who feels that he needs to keep a close watch over things.

MOORE GHOSTS GATHER IN VILLISCA

Villisca was once a bustling town in southwestern Iowa. In the early 1900s, it was home to more than 2,500 citizens, a busy train station, and dozens of businesses. But on June 10, 1912, a local family was brutally murdered in their home. The crime was never solved, and the town has since dwindled in size to about half as many residents. You might say that Villisca has become a ghost town...literally.

HOW IT ALL BEGAN—AND ENDED

The home of Josiah Moore and his wife, Sarah, was much like many other houses of its time. Built in 1868, it was a well-kept two-story white house on a quiet street in the heartland of America. After attending a Children's Day event on the night of June 9, 1912, the Moores and their four children, as well as Lena and Ina Stillinger— two young neighbor girls who were sleeping over— returned to the house and went to bed.

The next morning, Mary Peckham, the Moores' next-door neighbor, went outside to hang her laundry and was struck by the silence that greeted her from the Moore house; after all, a family of six was rarely quiet. Peckham called Josiah's brother Ross, who then came over to check things out.

BUNGLED BUNGALOW

Ross unlocked the door and entered the parlor; the home was covered in a blanket of eerie silence. But when he opened the door to one of the bedrooms, he was confronted with a horrific sight: the bloody bodies of the Stillinger girls lying in a bed.

Peckham called the police, who arrived to find the lifeless bodies of Josiah, Sarah, Herman, Katherine, Boyd, and Paul Moore, as well as the Stillinger girls—they had all been brutally murdered with an ax, which had been wiped off and left by the door of the downstairs bedroom.

That the crime was never solved is no real surprise due to the mayhem that ensued. As word of the carnage spread, friends and hundreds of curious onlookers raced to the house, where police soon lost control of the crime scene. With all of this chaos and none of today's technology, police were unable to solve the case—a fact that haunted them for the rest of their lives.

THE SUSPECTS

Among the leading suspects was Frank F. Jones, a local businessman who was angry with Josiah for leaving his company and poaching one of its best clients. People who believe in this theory suggest that Jones hired hit man William Mansfield to do the dirty work. Although police were suspicious of the pair, they did not find enough evidence to prosecute either of them.

Another school of thought suggests that a drifter committed the murders. Two men fit the bill: Andy Sawyer, a vagrant who traveled with an ax, and Henry Moore, who was later convicted of killing his mother and grandmother with an ax and was a suspect in several other ax murders. But no evidence connected either to the Villisca murders.

Traveling preacher George Kelly was another prime suspect. A rather odd character, Kelly had been present at the Children's Day event at the Moores' church. He left town the morning that the bodies were discovered and reportedly told fellow train passengers that he'd had a vision that told him to "Slay and slay utterly." When he was arrested for another crime in 1914, he admitted to the Moore murders but later withdrew his confession. Nevertheless, Kelly was tried twice for the Moore murders: One trial ended in a hung jury, and he was acquitted in the other.

IF YOU RENOVATE IT, THEY WILL COME

After the murders, the Moore house changed hands several times because, really, who wants to live in a house where eight people were killed? By 1994, the house was dilapidated and in danger of being torn down; that's when a realtor presented Darwin and Martha Linn with a proposal. The couple operated the Olson-Linn Museum in Villisca, and the realtor hoped that they'd be interested in purchasing the house to preserve another piece of the town's history; they were.

The Linns secured state funding to restore the house. Using old photographs, they remodeled and redecorated it with items from the early 1900s. They removed the electricity, water, and working bathrooms and restored the building to its 1912 condition. It was placed on the National Register of Historic Places in 1998.

After the renovation was complete, the Linns began giving tours of the house. On these tours, visitors get a glimpse of Villisca in the early 1900s and learn the details of the grisly murders. Other topics of discussion include possible suspects and how the crime and the eventual trial of Reverend Kelly affected the small town.

THEY'RE BAAAAACK

With the house looking almost exactly as it had in 1912, it seems that the spirits of the Moore family were drawn back to it. Visitors have reported seeing apparitions and hearing voices whisper in their ears. Closet doors open and close by themselves, and balls mysteriously roll across the floor.

Darwin Linn said that he always felt a pull toward this house, and he'd heard stories about the spirits that linger there. But when the renovations went smoothly, he dismissed the idea...until he saw the youngsters who came through the house on tours: He saw them interacting with other children—children who weren't there. "That makes the hair stand up on the back of my head," he said. That's when he became convinced that the Moore family is still around.

Many ghost hunters and paranormal investigators have toured the house and found evidence of spirits there. Orbs have been captured in photos and mysterious voices have been recorded on audio devices. But some of the most interesting documentation was collected by Maritza Skandunas, who related her harrowing firsthand account on the TV show *My Ghost Story.*

1912 AGAIN

Skandunas, the founder of San Diego Ghost Hunters, decided that if most people take tours of the Moore house, she'd like to go one step further and spend the night there. Darwin Linn said that he was a little surprised by the request, but he was open to the idea; he didn't even charge her for the lodging. So Skandunas and a couple of ghost-hunting friends settled in at the dark and primitive house. "It felt like you went back a hundred years," she said. "You could almost relive what they felt and the screaming that must have been going on, and no one heard it." Skandunas said that she felt that pure "evil was [permeating] out of the walls."

As Skandunas and her friends walked through the house absorbing the energy, they were able to imagine what took place in each room. Soon, they noticed a black shadow following them; they believe that it was the spirit of the murderer. Skandunas said that it gave off "a very hateful energy."

In the master bedroom, Skandunas felt something touch her arm; that sensation was validated when she took a picture of the room's mirror and saw the image of Sarah Moore staring back at her in the photo.

In one of the children's rooms, the investigators discovered the spirits of youngsters who were hoping to interact with the living. When they asked Herman, the eldest, to open the closet door, the door opened, even though no one was near it. When Skandunas's friend suggested reading one of the children's books aloud, the ghostly excitement was palpable. But shortly thereafter, the black shadow appeared and the reader began to feel nauseated. The killer obviously didn't want any happiness in the house, but when the group left the room, an audio recorder captured the voice of a child saying, "Don't go."

When the investigators asked the kids if they knew who committed the murders, they said no, but added clearly that it was two people. It seems that the Moores may have stuck around to offer clues about that terrible night.

EVIL ENERGY

Even a seasoned ghost hunter like Skandunas was shaken by the night's revelations. "I had goose bumps," she said. "I would never go into that house alone."

According to historical records, the town was named "Villisca" after a Native American word meaning "pleasant view." But others claim that the town was originally called "Wallisca," which means "evil spirit." Now that sounds about right.

THE BLACK ANGEL OF DEATH

The "Black Angel of Death" is unlike other angel statues at Oakland Cemetery in Iowa City, Iowa. For starters, at eight and a half feet tall (not including its pedestal), it towers high above the others. The eyes of the other angel statues gaze up toward heaven, and their wings are folded on their backs, which signals hope. But with its wings spread wide and pointing toward the ground, the Black Angel stares down upon the grave of Eddie Dolezal, who died in 1891 at age 18. The other angels are made of white marble; the Black Angel was sculpted out of bronze, which turned black over the years due to oxidation (or, as some speculate, the sins of Eddie's mother, who commissioned the statue in 1912). The Black Angel is different from the other angels in another important way: According to legend, it likes to take new victims.

DEATH IS IMMINENT

The Black Angel doesn't like to be touched inappropriately or witness public displays of affection. Locals know that girls should not be kissed near the statue: The consequence is death within six months. Anyone who touches the statue on Halloween night has only seven more years to live. Worse, giving the Angel a kiss can stop a person's heart.

The Black Angel is said to take its ultimate revenge on those who desecrate it. Legend says that four boys died in a car crash not long after urinating on the Black Angel. Another story tells of a young man who removed the thumb of the Angel; soon after, his body was found hundreds of miles away in the Chicago River, dead from strangulation. A single thumbprint was imprinted on his neck. Not long after, a bronze thumb, blackened with age, was reportedly found at the base of the Black Angel.

Whether or not the Black Angel has actually killed anyone is debatable, but photos do often reveal strange lights around it. One couple found that every one of their pictures featured a red light where the angel's heart would be. Other snapshots have included orbs, which signify the presence of spirits. For whatever reason, the Black Angel does not rest well. Anyone in its presence should beware of its powers.

ATCHISON, KANSAS: A TRUE GHOST TOWN

According to census records, approximately 10,000 people call Atchison, Kansas, home. While this is a good indication of how many people live in the town, it doesn't measure another important piece of data: how many ghosts reside there. Considering the ratio of ghosts to living residents, Atchison could quite possibly be the most haunted town in the United States.

MADAM OF THE MISSOURI RIVER

One of Atchison's oldest ghost stories traces its origin back more than a hundred years, when what is currently Atchison Street was called Ferry Street. This road travels down the side of a steep hill and ends at the Missouri River. In years past, the riverside site was used to board ferries, and legend has it that a woman lost control of her buggy and crashed into the water, where she drowned. Her lonely spirit supposedly tries to lure men into her watery grave.

MOURNFUL MOLLY OF JACKSON PARK

Jackson Park is the site of a purported haunting by a female spirit named Molly. One story suggests that Molly was a black woman who was lynched by a mob for having an affair with a white man. Another version indicates that Molly was a high-school girl who fought with her date on prom night, leaving his car in disgust and entering the park; the next morning, her body was supposedly found hanging from a tree with her dress torn and tattered. Other stories contend that after Molly's boyfriend broke up with her, she jumped to her death from a high ledge in the park. Whoever the female spirit is, she often moans and unleashes shrill screams in the park around midnight, and some claim that they have seen her ghostly figure hanging from a tree.

THE ABANDONED BABY OF BENEDICTINE COLLEGE

Two dorms at Benedictine College—a Catholic university founded in Atchison in 1858—are haunted: one by a baby and the other by one of the school's founding monks. The monks protect the school, and one has often been sighted at Ferrell Hall. The ghost-baby resides in Memorial Hall; legend has it that a female student once gave birth in the closet of her dorm room, but the newborn died. Several residents of Memorial Hall have reported feeling a phantom baby in their beds at night. Even more terrifying, one woman was trapped in her closet when a dresser mysteriously moved in front of the door while she was inside. Her roommate was not there, so she had to scream for help. Another student reported that her desk chair suddenly began to rock back and forth. And yet another woman awoke around 3 a.m. to see a shadowy figure going to and from her closet; in the morning, she discovered that her possessions had been tossed onto the floor.

DEAL WITH THE DEVIL

The Gargoyle Home on North Fourth Street is named for
the menacing gargoyles that decorate the facade of the
house, which is rumored to be cursed. The gargoyles were
supposedly built to honor the original owner's pact with
the devil; when a subsequent owner tried to remove the
gargoyles in an attempt to make the house more pleasant,
he fell to his death. In 2005, when the Travel Channel
sent a paranormal investigation team to Atchison, the
researchers equipment detected the presence of ghosts in
the building.

WHEN GHOSTS DON'T GET THEIR WAY...WATCH OUT!

Although every ghost story is unsettling in its own way,
a restless spirit at Sallie's House might just be the most
disturbing specter in a town full of them. This building on
North Second Street once served as a doctor's office; the
physician lived with his family upstairs and ran
his practice on the ground floor. One night in the
early 1900s, a girl named Sallie was brought
to the office. It is unclear whether she had a
severe respiratory infection or her appendix
burst, but in any event, she died.

Sallie's spirit seems to have been
reawakened in 1993, when a
couple moved into the house with
their young child. Sallie liked to
rearrange the child's toys while
the family was out,

turn appliances on and off, and move pictures so that they hung upside down.

But Sallie was not the only spirit in the house: Allegedly, another ghost physically attacked the husband. A psychic told the couple that this spirit was in her thirties and that she had fallen in love with the husband. (Sallie told the medium that she did not like this other ghost.) The malevolent spirit tried to turn the man against his wife, but when that didn't work, the entity became violent. Just before the jealous spirit attacked the man of the house, the room grew very cold. Then, suddenly, scratches and welts appeared on his arms, back, and stomach. After the ghost tried to push the man down the stairs, the couple moved out. The malevolent haunting stopped, but in 2005, audio recordings picked up the sounds of children playing while the house was empty.

CHAPTER 4

THE SOUTH

LINCOLN STILL LINGERS AT THE WHITE HOUSE

The Colonial-style mansion at 1600 Pennsylvania Avenue may be America's most famous residence, as well as one of the most haunted. Day and night, visitors and staff members have seen the spirits of past presidents, first ladies, and other former occupants. None of them are more celebrated than Abraham Lincoln, whose spirit is almost as powerful today as it was when he led America through the Civil War.

TWO WARTIME LEADERS MEET

During World War II, the Queen's Bedroom was called the Rose Room. While visiting the White House, Winston Churchill strolled into the Rose Room completely naked and smoking a cigar after taking a bath. It was then that he encountered the ghost of Abraham Lincoln standing in front of the fireplace with one hand on the mantle, staring down at the hearth. Always a quick wit, Churchill said, "Good evening, Mr. President. You seem to have me at a disadvantage."

According to Churchill, Lincoln smiled at him and then vanished. Churchill refused to stay in the Rose Room again, but Lincoln wasn't finished surprising guests.

LINCOLN DISTURBS THE QUEEN

When Queen Wilhelmina of the Netherlands stayed in the Queen's Bedroom in 1945, she was hoping to get a good night's sleep. Instead, she was awakened by noisy footsteps in the corridor outside her room. Annoyed, she waited for whomever it was to return to his or her room, but the individual stopped at her door and knocked loudly several times. When the queen finally opened the door, she found herself face to face with the specter of Abraham Lincoln. She said that he looked a bit pale but very much alive and was dressed in travel clothes, including a stovepipe hat and coat. The queen gasped, and Lincoln vanished.

Lincoln's ghost may be the most solid-looking and "real" spirit at the White House, and hundreds of people have encountered it. Strangely enough, Lincoln seemed to be in touch with the Other Side even before he died: He once claimed that he saw his own apparition and talked about it often.

HONEST ABE SEES HIS OWN GHOST

The morning after Abraham Lincoln was first elected president, he had a premonition about his death. He saw two reflections of himself in a mirror: One image showed how he usually appeared, fit and healthy; in the other, his face was pale and ghostly. Lincoln and his wife believed that the vision predicted that he wouldn't complete his second term in office.

Shortly before his assassination, Lincoln saw his own funeral in a dream. He said that he was in the White House, but it was strangely quiet and filled with mourners. Walking through the halls, he entered the East Room, where, to his horror, he saw a body wrapped in funeral vestments and surrounded by soldiers.

Lincoln said that in his dream, he approached one of the soldiers to find out what had happened. "Who is dead in the White House?" he demanded. "The president," the soldier replied. "He was killed by an assassin!"

A few days later—that fateful day when he attended Ford's Theatre for the last time—President Lincoln called a meeting of his cabinet members. He told them that they would have important news the following morning. He also explained that he'd had a strange dream...one that he'd had twice before. In it, he saw himself alone and adrift in a boat without oars. That was all he said, and the cabinet members left the president's office with a very uneasy feeling. The next day, they received the news that the president had been assassinated.

LINCOLN NEVER LEAVES

Hundreds of people have felt Lincoln's presence in the White House, and many have witnessed his apparition as well, including Eleanor Roosevelt's maid, who saw a spectral Abe sitting on a bed removing his boots. Franklin Roosevelt's valet ran out of the White House after encountering Lincoln's spirit, and Calvin Coolidge's wife saw Abe's face in a window in the Yellow Oval Room.

President Lincoln has been seen in many places in the White House, but he appears most frequently in the Lincoln Bedroom. Although the late president's bed is now in this room, during his lifetime, the space served as the cabinet room in which he signed the Emancipation Proclamation.

ABE'S OTHER HAUNTS

After his death, Lincoln's body was returned to his home state of Illinois to share a tomb with his sons Edward and Willie, who had preceded him in death. It took five years for a more elaborate tomb to be completed, and during that time, unexplainable things began to occur. Visitors reported seeing Lincoln's spirit roaming the area. And after the monument was erected, people heard sobs and footsteps coming from the spot. Cemetery workers had to move Lincoln's body several times to protect it from grave robbers, and to this day, footsteps and whispers can be heard near his final resting place. Perhaps the Great Emancipator wonders if his rest will be disturbed yet again.

Considering Lincoln's sensitivity to the supernatural world, it's not surprising that he would haunt Ford's Theatre, where he was fatally shot. Unfortunately, Lincoln's spirit has to share the stage with the ghost of his killer, John Wilkes Booth, who has also been spotted at the theater making his getaway. Another hot spot for ghostly sightings of Abraham Lincoln is Fort Monroe in Virginia—a Union stronghold that played a prominent role in the Civil War. Lincoln's specter has been seen there conferring with General Ulysses S. Grant over the Union's wartime strategy.

STEPHEN DECATUR'S GHOST

In Washington, D.C., a sullen figure stands at a window, looking at the world outside—even though he is a visitor from the Great Beyond. The figure is the ghost of Stephen Decatur, one of the country's greatest military heroes—long dead but condemned to prowl the halls of his former home.

RISING STAR

In 1807, Stephen Decatur was already a war hero for the young United States. He garnered accommodations for his bravery against the Barbary Pirates and for serving as a member of a naval commission that investigated the actions of Commodore James Barron. Barron was the commander of the U.S. frigate *Chesapeake;* after the British ship *Leopold* fired a shot across the *Chesapeake's* bow, Barron boarded the *Leopold* and took four of its sailors into custody. At the time, tensions between Britain and America were running high, so the commission on which Decatur served was organized to investigate Barron's actions.

It found that Barron had not received permission for his actions, so he was court-martialed and suspended for five years. Decatur spoke against Barron at the hearing, and Barron was not a man to forgive and forget.

When the War of 1812 broke out between the United States and England, Decatur took command of the *Chesapeake* and built up his reputation while Barron seethed on the sidelines. Then, in 1818, Decatur and his wife, Susan, became power players on the Washington, D.C., social scene after they built a house on fashionable Lafayette Square. However, Decatur's past would come back to haunt him. Over the years, Barron had unleashed a series of personal attacks on him. The whole affair culminated in early 1820 when Barron challenged Decatur to a duel.

FALLEN STAR

The night before the duel, Decatur stared glumly from his bedroom window, looking at his estate and the neighborhood. The next day, at a field in Maryland, Decatur—apparently channeling his inner Alexander Hamilton—attempted only to wound Barron (even though Decatur was an expert marksman). However, Barron— taking a page from Aaron Burr's playbook—shot to kill and mortally wounded his enemy. Decatur was carried home, where he died an agonizing death on March 22, 1820. While he lay dying, the heartbroken Susan could barely look at him because she was so upset.

ETERNAL STAR

Soon after his death, people began seeing a figure staring sadly out of the window where Decatur himself had stood on the night before the duel. The ghost was seen so often that eventually the window was sealed up. But bricks and mortar can't keep a good ghost down—Decatur's apparition continued to manifest throughout the house and at other windows.

Today, the former Decatur home is a museum of White House history. However, that has not stopped the ghost of Stephen Decatur from roaming its halls and appearing in various rooms, always with an expression of infinite sadness on his face.

Sometimes, in the early morning hours, a figure is spotted leaving the building through the back door. It carries a black box—perhaps containing a dueling pistol—just as Decatur did on the last day of his life. Inside the house, people have felt unbelievable sadness and emptiness in the first-floor room where Decatur died.

However, Stephen Decatur is not the only restless spirit that haunts the Lafayette Square property. Disembodied sobbing and wailing have been heard throughout the house; some speculate that it's the ghost of Susan Decatur reliving her life's greatest sorrow.

WAS THE EXORCIST REALLY BASED ON A TRUE STORY?

Almost everyone is familiar with the movie The Exorcist. *The 1973 film stars Ellen Burstyn, Jason Miller, and—most memorably—Linda Blair as a young girl who is possessed by a demon. Naturally, everyone wants to know if the story—which was based on a best-selling novel by William Peter Blatty—is true. The answer to that question is...maybe.*

IT BEGINS

In January 1949, a 13-year-old boy named Roland (some sources say that his name was Robbie) and his family—who lived in Mount Rainier, Maryland—began hearing scratching sounds from behind the walls and inside the ceiling of their house. Believing that their home was infested with mice, Roland's parents called an exterminator. However, the exterminator found no evidence of rodents in the house. After that, the family's problem got worse: They began to hear unexplained footsteps in the home, and objects such as dishes and furniture seemed to relocate on their own.

But these incidents would seem minor compared to what came next: Roland claimed that an invisible entity attacked him and that his bed shook so violently that he couldn't sleep. The sheets and blankets were repeatedly ripped from his bed and tossed onto the floor. One time, Roland tried to grab them, but he was yanked onto the floor with the bedcovers still clenched in his fists.

Roland liked board games, and his aunt Tillie—a woman who had a strong interest in the supernatural—had taught him how to use a Ouija board before she died. Some blamed the Ouija board for causing the trouble, claiming that it had allowed a demonic being to come into the home and target Roland.

NOT SUCH GOOD VIBRATIONS

By this time, the family was convinced that an evil entity was afoot, so they appealed to a Lutheran minister named Schulze for help. Reverend Schulze prayed for Roland and had his congregation do so as well. He even took Roland to his own home so the boy could get some sleep. However, both the bed and an armchair that Roland tried to sleep in there vibrated and moved, allowing the boy no rest. Schulze noted that Roland seemed to be in a trance while these incidents occurred.

If Schulze had any doubt that it was time to call in the cavalry, he was certainly convinced when scratches mysteriously materialized on Roland's body. These marks were then replaced by words that appeared to be made by claws. The word *Louis* was clearly visible, which was interpreted as St. Louis—Roland's mother's hometown. With all signs pointing to the need for an exorcism, Father Edward Albert Hughes of St. James Catholic Church was summoned.

TRUTH OR FICTION?

At this point, accounts of the story begin to splinter, as no two versions are alike. According to the version that has been more or less accepted as fact, Father Hughes went to see Roland and was disturbed when the boy addressed him in Latin—a language that was unknown to the youth. Hughes decided to perform an exorcism, during which a loose bedspring slashed him. The priest was supposedly so shaken by the ordeal that he was never the same again. (However, according to some sources, this part of the story never happened; they say that Hughes only saw Roland once at St. James, Roland never spoke in Latin, and Hughes never performed an exorcism on the boy, nor was he physically or emotionally affected by it. It is unclear why someone felt that dramatic license needed to be taken here, because the actual events are strange enough.)

During Roland's visit to Hughes, the priest suggested using blessed candles and special prayers to help the boy. But when Roland's mother did this, a comb flew across the room, hitting the candles and snuffing them out. Other objects also flew around the room, and at one point, a Bible was thrown at the boy's feet. Supposedly, Roland had to stop attending school because his desk shook so badly.

It seems that an attempt was made to baptize Roland into the Catholic faith as a way of helping him. However, this didn't work out so well: As his uncle drove him to the ceremony, the boy grabbed him by the throat and screamed that the baptism wouldn't work.

THE BATTLE OF ST. LOUIS

Finally, at their wits' end, the family decided to stay with relatives in the St. Louis area. Unfortunately, the distance between Maryland and Missouri proved to be no deterrent to the invisible entity, and the assaults on Roland continued.

In St. Louis, a relative introduced the boy and his family to Jesuit priest Father William Bowdern, who, in turn, employed Father Raymond J. Bishop, a pastor at St. Francis Xavier Church in St. Louis, in his efforts to help the family.

Father Bishop made several attempts to stop the attacks on the boy but to no avail. After Bishop sprinkled the boy's mattress with holy water in the shape of a cross, the attacks ceased. However, after Bishop left the room, the boy suddenly cried out in pain; when his pajama top was pulled up, Roland had numerous scratches across his abdomen. He could not have done it to himself, as he was in the presence of several witnesses at all times.

After more nights of violence against Roland, Father Bishop returned—this time with Father Bowdern. They prayed in the boy's room and then left. But as soon as they departed, loud noises began emanating from the room. When family members investigated, they found that an extremely heavy bookcase had swiveled around, a bench had overturned, and the boy's mattress was once again shaking and bouncing. It was at this point that another exorcism was deemed the only sensible course of action left.

The exorcism was a desperate battle that was waged over the course of several months. Some of it took place in the rectory at St. Francis Xavier Church, some of it at a hospital, and some of it at Roland's home; one source says that the boy was exorcised no less than 20 times. During this time, practically everything and anything typically associated with an exorcism occurred: Roland's body jerked in uncontrollable spasms, he experienced projectile vomiting, and he spit and cursed at the priests;

he also conveyed information that he couldn't possibly have known. However, his head didn't spin completely around like Linda Blair's did in *The Exorcist*.

GONE, BUT CERTAINLY NOT FORGOTTEN

Eventually, Bowdern's persistence paid off. He repeatedly practiced the ritual and ignored the torrent of physical and verbal abuse hurled at him by the entity that was residing inside the boy. Finally, in mid-April 1949, Roland spoke with a voice that identified itself as St. Michael. He ordered Satan and all demons to leave the boy alone. For the next few minutes, Roland went into a titanic rage, as if all the furies of the world were battling inside of him. Suddenly, he became quiet, turned to the priests, and simply said, "He's gone." The entity *was* gone, and fortunately, Roland remembered little about the ordeal. Some months later, a 20-year-old Georgetown University student named William Peter Blatty spotted an article in *The Washington Post* about Roland's experience. He let the idea of demonic possession percolate in his brain for years before finally writing his book, which became a best seller. Out of privacy concerns, Blatty changed so many details from the actual case that the source was virtually unrecognizable—until the intense publicity surrounding the movie forced the "real" story out.

Numerous theories regarding the incident have been suggested: Some say that it was an elaborate hoax gone too far, while others claim that it was the result of poltergeist activity or an actual possession. Regardless, this case continues to resonate in American culture.

AMERICA'S MOST HAUNTED LIGHTHOUSE

Built in 1830, the historic Point Lookout Lighthouse is located in St. Mary's County, Maryland, where the Potomac River meets Chesapeake Bay. It is a beautiful setting for hiking, boating, fishing, camping, and ghost-hunting.

THE MOST GHOSTS

Point Lookout Lighthouse has been called America's most haunted lighthouse, perhaps because it was built on what later became the largest camp for Confederate prisoners of war. Marshy surroundings, tent housing, and close quarters were a dangerous combination, and smallpox, scurvy, and dysentery ran rampant. The camp held more than 50,000 soldiers, and between 3,000 and 8,000 died there.

Park rangers and visitors to the lighthouse report hearing snoring and footsteps, having a sense of being watched, and feeling the floors shake and the air move as crowds of invisible beings pass by. A photograph of a former caretaker shows the misty figure of a young soldier leaning against the wall behind her, although no one noticed him when the photo was taken during a séance at the lighthouse. And a bedroom reportedly smelled like rotting flesh at night until the odor was publicly attributed to the spirits of the war prisoners.

THE LOST GHOST

In December 1977, Ranger Gerald Sword was sitting in the lighthouse's kitchen on a stormy night when a man's face appeared at the back door. The man was young, with a floppy cap and a long coat, and peered into the bright room. Given the awful weather, Sword opened the door to let him in, but the young man floated backward until he vanished entirely. Later, after a bit of research, Sword realized he had been face-to-face with Joseph Haney, a young officer whose body had washed ashore after the steamboat he was on sank during a similar storm in 1878.

THE HOST GHOST

One of Point Lookout's most frequent visitors is the apparition of a woman dressed in a long blue skirt and a white blouse who appears at the top of the stairs. She is believed to be Ann Davis, the wife of the first lighthouse keeper. Although her husband died shortly after he took the post, Ann remained as the keeper for the next 30 years, and, according to inspection reports, was known for clean and well-kept grounds. Caretakers claim to hear her sighing heavily.

WHO SAID THAT?

Point Lookout's reputation drew Hans Holzer, Ph.D., a renowned parapsychologist, who tried to capture evidence of ghostly activity. Holzer and his team claimed to have recorded 24 different voices in all, both male and female, talking, laughing, and singing. Among their recordings, the group heard male voices saying "fire if they get too close," "going home," and more than a few obscenities.

TAKE CARE, CARETAKER

One former caretaker reported waking in the middle of the night to see a ring of lights dancing above her head. She smelled smoke and raced downstairs to find a space heater on fire. She believes that the lights were trying to protect her and the lighthouse from being consumed by flames.

A FULL HOUSE

The lighthouse was decommissioned in 1966, after 135 years of service. In 2002, the state of Maryland purchased it, and it is now open for tours and paranormal investigations.

THE GHOSTS OF ANTIETAM

With nearly 23,000 total casualties, the Battle of Antietam was one of the bloodiest single-day skirmishes of the American Civil War. More than 3,600 of these men died suddenly and violently that day—ripped out of this world and sent reeling into the next. It's no wonder that the ghosts of some of these soldiers still haunt the Antietam battlefield in western Maryland. Perhaps they're still trying to understand what happened to them on that terrible day.

GAELIC GHOSTS

Bloody Lane at Antietam National Battlefield is a sunken road that's so named because of the incredible slaughter that took place there on September 17, 1862. One of the notable battalions that fought at Bloody Lane was the Union's Irish Brigade, which lost more than 60 percent of its soldiers that day. The brigade's Gaelic war cry was "faugh-a-ballaugh" (pronounced "fah-ah-bah-LAH"), which means "clear the way."

Many years ago, a group of schoolchildren took a class trip to Antietam. After touring the battlefield, several boys walked down Bloody Lane toward an observation tower that had been built where the Irish Brigade had charged into the battle. Later, back at the school, the boys wrote that they heard odd noises coming from a nearby field. Some said that it sounded like a chant; others, however, likened the sounds to the "fa-la-la-la-la" portion of the Christmas carol "Deck the Halls." Did the boys hear the ghostly battle cry of the Irish Brigade?

On another occasion, some battle reenactors were lying on the ground near the sunken road when they suddenly began hearing a noise that they were very familiar with—the sound of a regiment marching in full battle gear. Their experience as reenactors allowed them to pick out specific sounds, such as knapsacks, canteens, and cartridge boxes rattling and scraping. However, no matter how hard they looked, the men could see no marching soldiers. They concluded that the sounds were made by an otherworldly regiment.

PRYING EYES

Because of its strategic location on the battlefield, the Phillip Pry House was pressed into service as a makeshift hospital during the battle. Much misery took place there, including the death of Union General Israel B. Richardson, despite the loving care of his wife Frances. In 1976, the house was damaged by fire, and one day during the restoration, the wife of a park ranger met a woman dressed in Civil War-era attire coming down the stairs. She asked her husband who the woman was, but he had no knowledge of a woman in period clothes at the park.

Later, a woman was seen staring out an upstairs window in the room where General Richardson died. Nothing was particularly unusual about this...except that the room was being renovated at the time and didn't have a floor. Was it the ghost of Frances Richardson, still trying to take care of her dying husband?

Members of the construction crew that was working at the house decided that this was not the project for them and abandoned it immediately after sighting this female phantom. Disembodied footsteps have also been reported going up and down the home's stairs.

SCREAMING SPECTERS

The spirits of Antietam are not just confined to the battlefield. Injured Confederate soldiers were brought to St. Paul Episcopal Church in Sharpsburg, and sometimes, the sounds of the wounded screaming in agony can still be heard there. Mysterious lights have also been seen in the church tower.

A BRIDGE BETWEEN TWO WORLDS

Burnside Bridge was another scene of massive slaughter at Antietam, as Union troops repeatedly tried to take the tiny stone span only to be driven back by intense Confederate fire. Many of the soldiers who died there were quickly buried in unmarked graves near the bridge, and now it seems as if that arrangement wasn't to their liking. Many credible witnesses, including park rangers, have reported seeing blue balls of light floating near the bridge at night. The faint sound of a phantom drumbeat has also been heard in the vicinity.

Although the Battle of Antietam took place around 150 years ago, it seems that in some places, the battle rages on—and for some, it always will.

FORT DELAWARE PRISON HOSTS GHOSTS THROUGH THE AGES

Pea Patch Island. Sounds quaint, doesn't it? Hardly the name of a place that you'd imagine would host a military prison...or the ghosts of former inmates who still can't seem to escape, even in death. But then, the hardships and horrors that were experienced there might just trump the loveliness that the name suggests.

THE FORT'S PRISONERS

Shaped like a pentagon, Fort Delaware Prison was completed in 1859, just prior to the Civil War. With a moat surrounding its 32-foot-high walls, it was a very secure place to hold Confederate POWs.

With no extra blankets or clothing, Fort Delaware's inmates struggled to keep warm and suffered through the cold, harsh winters that are typical in the Mid-Atlantic region. Malaria, smallpox, and yellow fever were commonplace, and they traveled quickly through the facility; estimates suggest that between 2,500 and 3,000 people may have died there—and many tormented souls seem to remain.

NOW APPEARING...

One ghost that has been seen by many workers at the Fort Delaware Prison—which is now a living-history museum—is not the spirit of a prisoner at all: It's that of a former cook who now spends her time hiding ingredients from the current staff. Visitors have reported hearing a harmonica in the laundry area, where a ghost has been spotted threading buttons in a long string. In the officer's quarters, a spectral child is known to tug on people's clothes and a ghostly woman taps visitors on the shoulder. Books fall from shelves, and chandelier crystals swing back and forth by themselves.

And then there are the darker, more sinister spirits— the ones that suffered in life and found no relief in death. Moans, muffled voices, and rattling chains fill the basement with spooky sounds of prisoners past. The halls echo with noises that resemble the sounds of someone trying to break free from chains. Apparitions of Confederate soldiers have been seen running through the prison, and sailors have witnessed lights on shore where there were none. Screams and desperate voices plead for help, but so far, no one has been able to calm these restless souls.

GHOST HUNTER ENDORSED

If you're searching for proof that these ghosts are the real deal, check out a 2008 episode of *Ghost Hunters* that was shot at Fort Delaware. Jason Hawes, Grant Wilson, and their team of investigators found quite a bit of paranormal activity when they visited the old prison. In the basement's tunnels, they heard unexplained footsteps and voices, as well as something crashing to the ground. A thermal- imaging camera picked up the apparition of a man who appeared to be running away from the group. And in the kitchen, the investigators heard a very loud banging sound that seemingly came from nowhere.

IN THE SPIRIT OF THINGS

It's not *all* terror at the old prison. Today, Fort Delaware is part of a state park that's open to tourists and offers many special programs. One event that appeals to athletes and history buffs alike is the Escape from Fort Delaware triathlon: Each year when the starting musket blasts, participants reenact the escape route of 52 inmates who broke out of Fort Delaware Prison during the Civil War.

THE OTHER SIDE FOR POWs

During the Civil War, so much misery was experienced at Camp Sumter—a prison for captured Union soldiers near Andersonville, Georgia—that the absence of a haunting there would be remarkable. It only served as a POW camp for a little more than a year, but during that time, 13,000 Union soldiers died there. Captain Henry Wirz, who was in charge of the prison, was hanged after the war for conspiracy and murder. His angry spirit still wanders the compound, and many visitors have smelled a vile odor that they attribute to his ghost.

ST. LOUIS CEMETERY IS NUMBER ONE AMONG SPIRITS

In one of the most haunted cities in America, you're bound to find ghosts if you know where to look. And even if you don't, keep in mind that old buildings, new buildings, and cemeteries all attract restless spirits. Among the cemeteries in New Orleans, one is known as the most haunted of them all—St. Louis Cemetery No. 1.

LOOKING SPOOKY

When European immigrants first settled in New Orleans, they needed a place to bury their dead. Unfortunately in New Orleans, that isn't as easy as it sounds. The city lies below sea level, so anything buried (i.e., a coffin) eventually pops back up to the surface due to the water level. That's why the city is full of aboveground cemeteries where the dead are encased in tombs or vaults. So instead of the tiny tombstones you see in graveyards in other parts of the country, the cemeteries in New Orleans are full of structures that are large enough to hold a coffin (or several). Those cemeteries are known as cities of the dead.

Near the French Quarter, you'll find St. Louis Cemetery No. 1. Established in 1789, it's a beautiful place that's full of historical significance...and ghosts. In fact, many consider it the most haunted cemetery in the United States. Just the look of St. Louis Cemetery No. 1 is enough to send a shiver down your spine. That's probably why it has been featured in several Hollywood movies, including *Easy Rider* (1969) and *Interview with the Vampire* (1994).

New Orleans is known for its eclectic mix of cultures, and the variety of burial traditions on display at St. Louis Cemetery No. 1 showcase this. French, Irish, and Spanish settlers are among the earliest people who were buried there, and today, their marble tombs mix with crumbling rocks. The graveyard's narrow rows and winding paths lead to dead ends and confusion. It's no wonder that visitors report hearing eerie sounds surrounding them in this otherworldly place. Is it the wind? Or is it the sound of spirits filling the air with their weeping and moaning? Ghostly figures and phantom mists hover near the tombs. Some of the spirits are thought to be well-known people; others are anonymous but no less frightening.

DOWNCAST SPIRITS

One oft-seen spirit is "Henry," who gave the deed to his tomb to a lady friend to have on hand when he died. Unbeknownst to him, she sold the plot while he was still alive, and upon his death some years later, he was buried in a potter's field. To this day, Henry is seen wandering through the cemetery, perhaps searching for a better place to spend his eternal rest. Some say that he has even asked mourners if there would be room for him in their loved one's tomb.

And if you like animals, St. Louis Cemetery No. 1 is a place to meet a few pets that are quite low maintenance. Ghosts of dogs and cats wander along the rows. All are friendly and are thought to be pets that belonged to a 19th-century groundskeeper. They seem to be looking for their beloved master.

VOODOO RESIDES HERE

The most famous spirit at St. Louis Cemetery No. 1, however, is that of Marie Laveau. Considered the Voodoo Priestess of New Orleans, Laveau died in 1881, but her spirit still haunts these grounds. Some say that she comes alive each year on June 23 (St. John's Eve) to lead her Voodoo followers. Between these periods of resurrection, her spirit is often seen wearing a distinctive red-and-white turban with seven knots. And if you don't happen to spot her ghost, you might just hear her mumbling Voodoo curses. She has also been known to appear in feline form as a huge black cat; you'll recognize this specter by its glowing red eyes.

Those brave enough to approach Laveau's tomb will want to heed this ritual: Make three Xs on the tombstone, turn around three times, and then knock three times on the stone, and your wish will be granted. And whatever you do, be sure to leave an offering—you definitely don't want to anger the Voodoo Priestess.

NO GHOSTLY GROUPIE FOR THIS CELEB

Apparently, celebrities don't intimidate ghosts. Actor Charles S. Dutton has been in more than 80 films and TV shows—including *Rudy* (1993), *Roc*, and *The L Word*—but that didn't matter to one ghostly resident of St. Louis Cemetery No. 1. As Dutton recounted in an episode of *Celebrity Ghost Stories*, he was in New Orleans directing a movie in 2006, when he and his girlfriend decided to visit the old cemetery to look for the grave of Marie Laveau.

After much searching, they found the tomb and were admiring the many offerings in front of it when they noticed that a nearby grave—which was marked "Duplessy 1850"—had been broken open. The casket was pulled out and its lid was open about five inches. Pure curiosity made them look inside, where they saw a skeleton with a colorful scarf around its neck. Dutton decided to close the coffin and shove it back into the tomb so that it wasn't exposed to the elements. It was getting late by then and his girlfriend pleaded with him to leave, but he kept working.

Suddenly, the couple felt a presence behind them. They turned and saw a raggedly dressed man wearing the same scarf around his neck as the skeleton in the coffin. The two men made eye contact, and Dutton described the moment as feeling as though the man was looking straight through his soul. The man eventually turned around and walked away, but when Dutton tried to follow him, he simply turned a corner and vanished. Dutton was convinced that he and his girlfriend had just met Mr. Duplessy, the man into whose casket they had just peered.

MYRTLES PLANTATION: A BLAST FROM THE PAST

Listed on the National Register of Historic Places and boasting more than 200 years of history, the Myrtles Plantation is a beautiful and sprawling old home in St. Francisville, Louisiana. Now used as a bed-and-breakfast, the mansion has seen its share of drama, including romance, death, and even murder. What better setting for a good old Southern-style haunting? Paranormal experts and amateur ghost hunters all agree that the Myrtles Plantation is one of the most haunted places in America.

TALES TO TELL

In 1796, David Bradford built what would eventually become the Myrtles Plantation on 650 acres of land about 30 miles outside of Baton Rouge. At the time, the house—which was originally known as Laurel Grove—was much smaller than it is today. In 1834, Ruffin Stirling purchased and remodeled the plantation, doubling its size and renaming it after the many myrtle trees on the property.

Over the years, many people lived and died at the Myrtles Plantation, so it's not surprising that the place is home to a few restless spirits. Whether it's strange noises, disembodied voices, apparitions, or reflections in a haunted mirror, plenty of paranormal activity can be found at Myrtles Plantation.

In 2005, investigators from the television show *Ghost Hunters* paid a visit to the mansion and documented several strange phenomena. Thermal-imaging video cameras recorded the torso of something not really present, as well as a shadow that appeared to be moving up and down. The team also caught the unexplained movement of a lamp across a table: Over the course of a few minutes, it moved several inches with no help from anyone in the room.

If you visit the Myrtles Plantation, be sure to check out the Myrtles mirror: It is said to reflect the spirit of someone who died in front of it. People have repeatedly seen handprints on the mirror and orbs or apparitions in photos of it. Although many stories say that the images belong to one of the plantation's early owners and her children—all of whom were poisoned—the mirror was actually brought to the house in the 1970s. If it is indeed haunted, the ghosts may not be from the home originally.

A SPIRITED PLACE

Several ghosts are commonly seen inside the house. One is thought to be a French woman who wanders from room to room. Another is a regular at the piano; unfortunately, this spirit only seems to know one chord, which is heard over and over, stopping suddenly when anyone walks into the room. A third is the ghost of a young girl, who only appears right before thunderstorms.

The spirits of two young girls have also been seen playing outside on the veranda, and guests have also felt their presence at night while lying in bed. Sometimes, visitors feel pressure on the bed, as though someone is jumping on it. Soon after, people report seeing the spirit of a maid, who appears to smooth the covers. Another young girl with long curly hair has been seen floating outside the window of the toy room; she appears to be cupping her hands as if she's trying to see inside.

Some visitors report seeing a Confederate soldier on the porch; others have seen the spirit of a man that warns them not to go inside. Many people have glimpsed apparitions of slaves doing their chores inside the mansion. And two other resident ghosts that are certainly entertaining but have little connection to the plantation's rich history are those of a ballet dancer clad in a tutu and a Native American woman who appears naked in the outdoor gazebo.

The ghost of William Winter is also said to haunt the mansion. Winter lived at the Myrtles Plantation from 1860 to 1868 and again from 1870 until his death in 1871, when an unknown assailant shot him as he answered the door. By some accounts, he staggered back inside and died on the 17th step of the staircase, where his slow dragging footsteps can be heard to this day.

CHLOE

Perhaps the best-known ghost at the Myrtles Plantation is that of Chloe, a former slave. Her spirit is thought to walk between the main house and the old slave quarters. People describe her apparition as that of a slender woman wearing a green turban.

As the story goes, David Bradford's daughter Sara married Clark Woodruff, who—it is rumored—had an affair with a beautiful slave girl named Chloe. After enjoying her station in the main house, Chloe was upset when Woodruff ended the affair. When he later caught her eavesdropping, Woodruff became enraged and cut off her ear. (It is said that she wears the green turban to cover the scar.) Two versions of the next part of this story exist: One has Chloe seeking revenge on Woodruff by poisoning his family; the other says that she poisoned them to secure her position as a nursemaid and nanny, so that she would be needed inside to nurse the family back to health, and therefore, she wouldn't be sent to work in the fields.

In either case, Chloe allegedly crushed up oleander petals and added them to a cake she was baking for the oldest daughter's birthday. Clark Woodruff didn't eat any of it, but his wife and two daughters did, and they soon died from poisoning. The other slaves, fearing punishment, dragged Chloe to the yard, where she was hanged. Legend has it that her ghost can be seen in the yard and wandering through the house in her signature headwear.

It's a great story, and it's easy to see why it would be repeated—and possibly twisted a bit each time. But researchers who have dug through old court records have found no evidence that there ever was a Chloe: There is nothing to suggest that a slave by that name (or anything close to it) ever lived at Myrtles Plantation. And although death records show that Sara Woodruff and two of the children did die young, all the deaths were attributed to yellow fever, not poison.

So there you have it. Myrtles Plantation is rife with ghosts, but we may never know exactly who they were in life or why they're still attached to the mansion. Chloe may or may not have existed in the real world, but you never know what you may encounter at one of the most haunted houses in America.

THE BELL WITCH OF TENNESSEE

There is perhaps no haunting in America that resonates quite like the event that occurred on the farm of John Bell in rural Tennessee. The story stands unique in the annals of folklore as one of the rare cases in which a spirit not only injured the residents of a haunted house but also caused the death of one of them! For this reason, even though the haunting occurred in the early 1800s, it has not yet been forgotten.

The story of the Bell Witch will be forever linked to the small town of Adams in northwestern Tennessee. In 1804, John Bell, his wife, Lucy, and their six children came to the region from North Carolina. He purchased 1,000 acres of land on the Red River, and the Bell family settled quite comfortably into the community. John Bell was well liked and kind words were always expressed about Lucy, who often opened her home to travelers and hosted social gatherings.

BUMPS IN THE NIGHT

The Bell haunting began in 1817 after John Bell and his son Drew spotted odd creatures in the woods near their farm. When they shot at the strange beasts, they vanished.

Soon after, a series of weird knocking, scraping, and scratching sounds began on the exterior of the house and then at the front door. Shortly thereafter, the sounds moved inside and seemed to emanate from the bedroom belonging to the Bell sons. This continued for weeks, and before long, the irritating sounds were heard all over the house. They continued from room to room, stopping when everyone was awake and starting again when they all went back to bed.

The Bells also heard what sounded like a dog pawing at the wooden floor or chains being dragged through the house. They even heard thumps and thuds, as though furniture was being overturned. These sounds were frightening, but not as terrifying as the noises that followed—the smacking of lips, gurgling, gulping, and choking—sounds seemingly made by a human. The nerves of the Bell family were starting to unravel as the sounds became a nightly occurrence.

THE COMING OF THE WITCH

The disembodied sounds were followed by unseen hands. Items in the house were broken and blankets were yanked from the beds. Hair was pulled and the children were slapped and poked, causing them to cry in pain. The Bells' daughter Betsy was once slapped so hard that her cheeks stayed bright red for hours.

Whatever the cause of this unseen force, most of its violent outbursts were directed at Betsy. She would often run screaming from her room in terror as the unseen hands prodded, pinched, and poked her. Strangely, the force became even crueler to her whenever she entertained her young suitor, Joshua Gardner, at the house. Desperately seeking answers, John Bell enlisted the help of some of his neighbors to investigate.

Even in the presence of these witnesses, the strange sounds continued, chairs overturned, and objects flew about the room. The neighbors formed an investigative committee, determined to find a cause for the terrifying events.

Regardless, the household was in chaos. Word began to spread of the strange happenings, and friends and strangers came to the farm to witness it for themselves. Dozens of people heard the banging and rapping sounds and chunks of rock and wood were thrown at curious guests by unseen hands.

As the investigative committee searched for answers, they set up experiments, tried to communicate with the force, and kept a close eye on the events that took place. They set up overnight vigils, but the attacks only increased in intensity. Betsy was treated brutally and began to have sensations that the breath was being sucked out of her body. She was scratched and her flesh bled as though she was being pierced with invisible pins and needles. She also suffered fainting spells and often blacked out for 30 to 40 minutes at a time.

Soon, a raspy whistling sound was audible, as if someone was trying to speak. It progressed until the force began to talk in a weak whisper. The voice of the force told them that it was a spirit whose rest had been disturbed, and it made many claims as to its origins, from being an ancient spirit to the ghost of a murdered peddler.

The excitement in the community grew as word spread that the spirit was communicating. People came from far and wide to hear the unexplained voice. Hundreds of people witnessed the activity caused by the witch. There were those who came to the Bell farm intent on either driving out the witch or proving that the entire affair was a hoax. But without fail, each of them left the farm confessing that the unusual events were beyond their understanding.

A STRANGE AFFLICTION

John Bell began to complain of a curious numbness in his mouth that caused his tongue to swell so greatly that he was unable to eat or drink for days at a time. As the haunting progressed, he began to suffer other inexplicable symptoms, most notably bizarre facial tics that rendered him unable to talk or eat and often made him lose consciousness. These odd seizures lasted from a few hours to a week, and they increased in severity as time wore on.

No one knows why John Bell was targeted by the spirit, but from the beginning, the witch made it clear that it would torment him for the rest of his life. Bell was also physically abused by the witch and many witnesses recalled him being slapped by unseen hands or crying out in pain as he was stabbed with invisible pins. Bell's doctor was helpless when it came to finding a cure for his ailments. The witch laughed at his efforts and declared that no medicine could cure him.

Some believe the reason for Bell's suffering was revealed one night when the spirit claimed to belong to Kate Batts, an eccentric neighbor who had disliked Bell because of some bad business dealings in the past. Whether the spirit was Batts is unknown, but people began calling the witch Kate.

THE DEATH OF JOHN BELL

By 1820, John Bell's physical condition had worsened. His facial jerks and twitches continued, as did the swelling of his tongue and the seizures that left him nearly paralyzed for hours or days at a time. In late October, he suffered another fit and took to his bed. He would never leave the house again. As Bell writhed in pain, Kate remained nearby, laughing and cursing at the dying man.

On the morning of December 19, 1820, Lucy checked on her husband who appeared to be sleeping soundly. An hour later, she returned to the bedroom and realized that he was in a stupor. When John, Jr., went to get his father's medicine, he discovered that all of his father's prescriptions had vanished. In place of them was a small vial that contained a dark-colored liquid. No one knew what had happened to the medicines or what was in the vial.

Suddenly, Kate's voice took over the room. She claimed that she had poisoned Bell with the contents of the dark vial and that he would never rise from his bed again.

The mysterious liquid was tested on a family cat, and the animal was dead in seconds.

John Bell never did recover. On December 20, he took one last shuddering breath and died. Laughter filled the house as the witch stated that she hoped John Bell would burn in hell. Bell was laid to rest in a small cemetery, a short distance from the family home. As mourners left the cemetery, the voice of Kate returned, echoing loudly in the cold morning air. She cheered the death of the man she hated so much. This ended the most terrifying chapter of a haunting that left an indelible mark in the annals of supernatural history. But the Bell Witch was not finished— at least not quite yet.

THE BROKEN ENGAGEMENT

After the funeral, the activities of the witch seemed to subside, but she was not totally gone. Kate remained with the family throughout the winter and spring of 1821, but she was not quite as vicious as she had been, not even to Betsy, around whom her activities continued to be centered.

During the haunting, it was clear that Betsy would be punished as long as she allowed herself to be courted by Joshua Gardner. But Betsy and Joshua refused to give in to Kate's wishes. In fact, on Easter Sunday 1821, the couple became engaged, much to the delight of their family and friends. But their joy would not last long as the antics of the witch returned with horrific force. Realizing that the witch would never leave her alone as long as she stayed with Joshua, Betsy broke off the engagement and never saw him again.

THE RETURN OF THE WITCH

In the summer of 1821, the witch left the Bell family, promising to return in seven years. In 1828, she came back and announced her return in the same manner as when the original haunting first began—scratching and other eerie sounds inside and outside the house, objects moving, and blankets pulled from the beds.

The Bells decided to ignore the activity, and, if spoken to by the spirit, they ignored it as well. In this way, they hoped the visitation might end quickly. And so it did— the witch left the house after a few weeks.

However, much of the activity during the witch's 1828 visit took place at the home of John Bell, Jr., who had built a house on land that he had inherited from his father. The witch allegedly made several accurate predictions about the future, including the Civil War, the end of slavery, the rise of the United States as a world power, and the coming of World Wars I and II. She even predicted the end of the world, stating that the world would end with the temperature of the planet rising so high that it would become uninhabitable.

Kate stayed with John Bell, Jr., for several months. Before she left, she promised to return again in 107 years (1935), and though there is no record that she ever did so, there are some that maintain that the Bell Witch has never left Adams, Tennessee. Strange events still occur where the old Bell farm stood. Old Kate is still talked about today and you'd have to travel far to find someone who does not believe that something very strange occurred there in the early 1800s. What was it exactly? No one knows for sure, but there's no question that it made an indelible mark on American history.

"LOTZ" OF GHOSTS GATHER AT CARTER HOUSE

Franklin, Tennessee, which is located about 20 miles south of Nashville, has a population of 64,000—unless you count its ghosts. The site of what some historians consider the bloodiest one-day battle of the Civil War, Franklin is rich with history—and restless spirits. It seems that many of the soldiers who lost their lives in that famous battle are still hanging around the city.

BEFORE THE BLOOD

In 1830, Fountain Branch Carter built a beautiful home in the heart of Franklin. In 1858, Johann Lotz constructed his own house across the street on land that he'd purchased from Carter. Both were blissfully unaware of what would occur there just a few years later.

After the fall of Nashville in 1862, Franklin became a Union military post. In 1864, in an attempt to "take the bull by the horns," the Confederate army decided to attack the enemy head-on in Franklin, hoping to drive General Sherman's army north. It didn't quite work out that way; instead, during the Battle of Franklin on November 30, 1864, more than 4,000 lives were lost, and because the battlefield was small, the concentration of bloodshed was very high. And most of it took place right in front of the Lotz and Carter homes.

THE BATTLE BEGINS

When the Confederate troops arrived in town, Union General Jacob Cox commandeered the Carter House as his base of operations. Fearing for their lives, the Carter family took refuge in the basement during the five long hours of the battle. In all, 23 people—including the Lotz family—crowded into the cellar. They all survived, and when the fighting was over, both houses were converted into field hospitals. Surgeries, amputations, and death filled the days and weeks that followed. Between the violence and the chaos, it's no wonder that some of the dead never found peace.

One of the men who was killed during the battle was Tod Carter, Fountain's son and a Confederate soldier who was thrilled to be heading home. He was wounded just 300 feet from his front door and was taken to his sister's bedroom, where he later died. Some say that his spirit remains there today.

HISTORY COMES TO LIFE

In 1953, the Carter House was opened to the public. Today, it's a museum and a National Historic Landmark; its eight acres stand as a tribute to the battle that took place there so long ago. If you look closely, more than a thousand bullet holes can be found on the property. The Lotz House—which was added to the National Historic Register in 1976 and opened to the public in 2008—

bears its share of scars as well: Bloodstains are evident throughout, and a round indentation in the wood floor is a reminder of a cannonball that crashed through the roof and flew through a second-floor bedroom before landing in the parlor on the first floor, leaving a charred path in its wake.

IN THE SPIRIT OF THINGS

Visitors to the Carter House have reported seeing the specter of Tod Carter sitting on a bed or standing in the hallway. His sister Annie has also been spotted in the hallways and on the stairs. She's blamed for playful pranks such as rolling a ball along the floor and causing objects to appear and disappear. But then again, the mischief-maker might be the spirit of one of the children who took refuge in the cellar during the battle. After all, staff members and visitors have reported feeling the sensation of a child tugging at their sleeves, and one worker saw a spectral child walking down the staircase.

The ghosts of soldiers and other family members may be responsible for some of the other unusual phenomena experienced in the house, such as furniture moving on its own, doors slamming, and apparitions peering through the windows. Not to be outdone, the ghosts at the Lotz House manifest as phantom voices and household items that move on their own or come up missing. While they haven't been identified, they seem to be civilian spirits rather than military ones. It's tough sharing space with so many ghosts, but the staff members are used to it, and they're happy to share the history—and the spirits—with visitors who stop by on the Franklin on Foot Ghost Tour. And don't worry:

These lively spirits have never followed anyone home—
at least not yet!

UNSETTLED SPIRITS AT THE SANATORIUM

*It was designed to save lives at a time when an epidemic
was sweeping the nation. Little did its developers know that
they were erecting a building in which scores of people
would take their last gasping breaths. Is it any wonder
that the halls of the Waverly Hills Sanatorium in Louisville,
Kentucky, still echo with the footsteps of those who
died there?*

ORIGINS

Around 1883, the first building was erected on the site of
what is now the Waverly Hills Sanatorium. Major Thomas
Hays, the owner of the property, decided that the local
schools were too far away for his daughters to attend, so
he constructed a small schoolhouse on the land and hired
teacher Lizzie Harris to instruct the girls. Because of her
love of Walter Scott's *Waverley* novels, Harris named the
place Waverly School. Taken by the name, Hays decided
to call his property Waverly Hill.

In the early 1900s, an outbreak of tuberculosis spread
across the United States. In an effort to confine the highly
contagious disease, the construction of TB sanatoriums and
hospitals was planned. In 1908, the Board of Tuberculosis
Hospitals purchased the Hays property, and in July 1910,
a small two-story building was opened; it had the capacity
to house nearly 50 patients.

THEY JUST KEEP COMING...

Without a cure in existence or any way to slow the disease, little could be done for TB patients at the time. Treatment often consisted of nothing more than fresh air and exposure to heat lamps. More and more patients arrived at the sanatorium; therefore, in the 1920s, expansion of the facility began, and in 1926, the building that stands today opened. This massive five-story structure could house nearly 400 patients. But once again, the rooms quickly filled up. The sad truth was that the sanatorium was only kept from overcrowding due to the fact that, without a cure, many of the patients died. Just how many people passed away there is the stuff of urban legends—some estimates go as high as 65,000. In truth, the number is probably closer to 8,000, but that's still a staggering number when one realizes that tuberculosis causes patients to slowly and painfully waste away over the course of weeks or even months.

In the 1940s, treatments for TB were introduced, and as a result, the number of patients at Waverly Hills consistently declined until the building was officially shut down in 1961.

THE FINAL YEARS

A short time later, Waverly Hills was reopened as the Woodhaven Geriatric Center. This chapter of the building's history came to an end around 1980 amid whispers of patient cruelty and abuse. Before long, those whispers became full-blown urban legends involving depravities such as electroshock therapy. Not surprisingly, it wasn't long before people started saying that the abandoned, foreboding structure was haunted.

MEET THE GHOSTS

So who are the ghosts that are said to haunt Waverly Hills? Sadly, the identities of most of them are unknown, but many of them have been encountered. Almost every floor of the building has experienced paranormal activity, such as disembodied voices and ghostly footsteps. Doors have been known to open and close by themselves, and bits of debris have been thrown at unsuspecting visitors. It is said that all one has to do is wait quietly to spot one of the many shadow people that walk down the hallways. Of course, if you're looking for a more interactive ghost encounter, you can always head up to the third floor. There, you might find the spirit of a young girl in the solarium. If she's not there, check the nearby staircases— apparently she likes to run up and down them.

Waverly Hills is also home to the ghost of a young boy who likes to play with a small ball that sometimes appears on the floor. Not wanting to wait to find the ball, some visitors have resorted to bringing their own, which they leave in a certain spot, only to see it roll away or even vanish before it appears on a different floor altogether.

WELCOME TO ROOM 502

Of all the allegedly haunted areas at Waverly Hills, none holds a candle to Room 502. Most of the legends associated with the room center on two nurses, both of whom supposedly committed suicide on the premises.

One nurse is said to have killed herself in the room in 1928. Apparently, she was a single woman who discovered that she was pregnant. Feeling that she had nowhere to turn, the young woman chose to slip a rope around her neck and hang herself. The other nurse who worked in Room 502 is said to have killed herself in 1932 by jumping from the roof, although the reason why is unclear. Although no documentation substantiating either of these suicides has been unearthed, that has not stopped visitors to Room 502 from experiencing paranormal activity. Upon entering the room, people often report feeling "heavy" or the sensation of being watched. It is quite common for guests to witness shadow figures darting around the room, and occasionally, a lucky visitor catches a glimpse of a spectral nurse standing by the window.

THE BODY CHUTE

When expansion of the building began in the 1920s, a rather morbid (though some would say essential) part of the sanatorium was constructed: the Body Chute— a 500-foot-long underground tunnel leading from the main building to a nearby road and set of railroad tracks. Some believe that the tunnel was created simply for convenience, while others think it was designed to prevent patients from seeing the truth—that many of them were dying. Although it was called a chute, bodies were never dumped into it; rather, they were walked through it

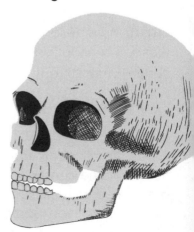

on gurneys. The tunnel was even equipped with a motorized cable system to help with transportation.

People walking through the Body Chute have reported hearing disembodied voices, whispering, and even painful groans. Sometimes, shadowy figures are seen wandering through the tunnel. But because the only light down there comes from random air vents, the figures vanish almost as quickly as they appear.

LIGHTS, CAMERA, GHOSTS!

After the TV show *Scariest Places on Earth* featured Waverly Hills in a 2001 episode, numerous programs began filming at the sanatorium. *Ghost Hunters* visited there twice—once in 2006 and again in 2007 as part of its annual live Halloween investigation. *Most Haunted* came all the way from the UK in 2008, and *Ghost Adventures* spent a night locked inside the sanatorium in 2010. But of all the episodes filmed at Waverly Hills, none was more bizarre than that of the short-lived VH1 show *Celebrity Paranormal Project.*

The series' debut episode, which aired in October 2006, was shot at Waverly Hills and featured actor Gary Busey, comedian Hal Sparks, *Survivor* winner Jenna Morasca, model/actress Donna D'Errico, and model Toccara Jones conducting an investigation. The supernatural activity began early in the evening, shortly after Busey and Morasca were sent to Room 418 to investigate. They weren't there long before their thermal-imaging camera picked up shapes moving around the room and even sitting on a bed near them. When Morasca was left in the room alone, she heard all sorts of strange noises and even encountered a small red ball, which wasn't there when the team first entered the room.

When Sparks was in the solarium, he rolled balls across the floor in an attempt to convince the spirits to play with him. The footage shows what appears to be one of the balls rolling back to him. At around the same time, Sparks reported seeing a small black shape—like that of a child—run past the doorway. Later on in the evening, D'Errico reported feeling that someone was following her, an incident that was accompanied by the sound of footsteps. She also heard what sounded like people screaming. She was so frightened that she ran away from the building screaming. Once back in the company of the other investigators, D'Errico said that she actually saw the figure of a man standing in a hallway. The evening ended with the entire group attempting to contact the spirits in Room 502. As they asked questions, banging noises and footsteps were heard coming from all around them. When they left the building, they were still hearing noises and encountered a child's ball that seemed to appear from out of nowhere.

MCRAVEN HOUSE: THE MOST HAUNTED HOUSE IN DIXIE?

Located near Vicksburg, Mississippi, the McRaven House was haunted even before it became a Civil War hospital.

The oldest parts of the estate known as McRaven House were built in 1797. Over the next 40 years, its owners gradually added to the property until it became a classic southern mansion, standing proudly among the magnolia blossoms and dogwood trees of the Old South.

And like nearly all such mansions, it has its share of resident ghosts. Today, McRaven House is often referred to as "the most haunted house in Mississippi." Some researchers believe that environmental conditions on the property make it particularly susceptible to hauntings: Ghosts that may not be noticeable in drier, less humid climates seem to be more perceptible in the dews of the delta. Of course, it helps that the McRaven House has seen more than its share of tragedy and death during its 200-year history.

THE GHOST OF POOR MARY

In the early 1860s, the house's supernatural activity seemed to center on an upstairs bedroom in which Mary Elizabeth Howard had died during childbirth in 1836 at age 15. Mary's brown-haired apparition is still seen descending the mansion's grand staircase. Her ghost is blamed for the poltergeist activity—such as pictures falling from the wall—that is often reported in the bedroom where she died. And her wedding shawl, which is occasionally put on display for tourists, is said to emit heat.

GHOSTS OF THE CIVIL WAR

Mary Elizabeth's ghost alone would qualify McRaven House as a notably haunted reminder of Mississippi's antebellum past, but she is far from the only spirit residing there, thanks in part to the bloody atrocities of the Civil War.

The Siege of Vicksburg, which took place in 1863, was one of the longest, bloodiest battles of the entire conflict. When General Ulysses S. Grant and his Union forces crossed the Tennessee River into Mississippi, Confederate forces retreated into Vicksburg, which was so well guarded that it was known as a "fortress city." But as more and more Union forces gathered in the forests and swamps around Vicksburg, Confederate General John C. Pemberton was advised to evacuate. Fearing the wrath of the local population if he abandoned them, Pemberton refused.

By the time the siege began in earnest, the Confederate troops were greatly outnumbered. Rebel forces surrendered the city of Vicksburg on July 4, 1863, after more than a month of fighting. Nearly all of the Confederate soldiers involved in the battle—around 33,000 in all—were captured, wounded, or killed. The Union victory put the entire Mississippi River in northern hands, and combined with the victory at Gettysburg that same week, it marked the beginning of the end for the Confederacy.

CAPTAIN MCPHERSON'S LAST REPORT

In the middle of the action stood McRaven House. In the early days of the siege, it served as a Confederate hospital, and, at that time, it was full of the screams of anguished and dying men. Cannons from both armies shot at the mansion, destroying large portions of it.

Later, after Union forces captured the house, it served as the headquarters for General Grant and the Union army. One of the officers put in charge of the house was Captain McPherson, a Vicksburg native who had fled to the North to fight for the Union. Sometime during the siege, he disappeared. Soon after, according to legend, McPherson's commanding officer awoke to find the captain in his room. He was furious at the intrusion until he noticed McPherson's mangled, bloody face and torn uniform. The commanding officer then realized that this was not McPherson himself—it was his ghost, which had returned to deliver the message that Rebels, who couldn't forgive him for abandoning the South, had murdered him. McPherson's ghost reputedly still wanders the grounds dressed in Union blue with blood oozing from a bullet wound in his forehead.

OTHER CIVIL WAR GHOSTS

Nearly a year after the siege ended, John Bobb—the owner of McRaven House at the time—spotted six Union soldiers picking flowers in his garden. Outraged by the trespassers, Bobb threw a brick at them and hit one of the Yankees in the head. After going to the local field commander to report the intruders, Bobb returned home to find 25 Union soldiers waiting for him; they marched him into the nearby bayou and shot him to death. His ghost has been seen roaming the property ever since.

THE WAR ENDED, BUT THE GHOSTS KEPT COMING

Mary Elizabeth and the Civil War-era ghosts aren't the only spirits that haunt McRaven House. In 1882, William Murray purchased the home, and over the next 78 years, five members of his family died on the premises. The most recent death there was that of his daughter Ella, who spent her last years as a recluse in the house, where she reportedly burned furniture to stay warm. After her death in 1960, the mansion was restored, refurbished, and opened for tours and battle reenactments. In the early morning hours, tour groups and staffers have often spotted the ghosts of Ella and the other Murrays who died in the house.

THE MOST HAUNTED HOUSE IN THE SOUTH?

Today, visitors can tour the McRaven House in all of its antebellum glory. Extensive collections of 19th-century furnishings, artwork, jewelry, and other artifacts are displayed at the mansion, and several ghosts from both sides of the Civil War are believed to share the house with Mary Elizabeth and the other spirits from the mansion's past. Ghost hunters have been conducting investigations at the house since at least the 1980s, and they've frequently photographed mysterious forms outside the building, often around the portion of the property that served as a burial ground for soldiers; some are simply odd blobs of light, but others appear to be human-shaped forms.

RIDDLES OF THE RIDDLE HOUSE

While functioning as a cemetery caretaker's home, West Palm Beach's Riddle House was always close to death. Since then, it's been relocated and repurposed, and now it sees its fair share of life—life after death, that is.

THE "PAINTED LADY"

Built in 1905 as a gatekeeper's cottage, this pretty "Painted Lady" seemed incongruent with the cemetery it was constructed to oversee. Cloaked in grand Victorian finery, the house radiated the brightness of life. Perhaps that's what was intended: A cemetery caretaker's duties can be gloomy, so any bit of spirit lifting would likely be welcomed. Or so its builders thought. In the case of this particular house, however, "spirit lifting" took on a whole new meaning.

The first ghost sighted in the area was that of a former cemetery worker named Buck, who was killed during an argument with a townsperson. Shortly thereafter, Buck's ghost was seen doing chores around the cemetery and inside the cottage. Luckily, he seemed more interested in performing his duties than exacting revenge.

In the 1920s, the house received its current name when city manager Karl Riddle purchased it and took on the duty of overseeing the cemetery. During his tenure, a despondent employee named Joseph hung himself in the attic. This sparked a frenzy of paranormal phenomena inside the house, including the unexplained sounds of rattling chains and disembodied voices. After Riddle moved out, the reports of paranormal activity slowed down—but such dormancy wouldn't last.

TRAVELING SPIRITS

By 1980, the Riddle House had fallen into disrepair and was abandoned. The city planned to demolish the building but instead decided to give it to John Riddle (Karl's nephew). He, in turn, donated it for preservation. The entire structure was moved—lock, stock, and barrel— to Yesteryear Village, a museum devoted to Florida's early years. There, it was placed on permanent display as an attractive token of days long past. There, too, its dark side would return—with a vengeance.

When workers began to reassemble the Riddle House, freshly awakened spirits kicked their antics into high gear. Ladders were tipped over, windows were smashed, and tools were thrown to the ground from the building's third floor. Workers were shocked when an unseen force threw a wooden board across a room, striking a carpenter in the head. The attacks were blamed on the spirit of Joseph, and the situation became so dangerous that work on the structure was halted for six months. After that, however, the Riddle House was restored to its previous glory.

GHOSTLY UNVEILING

During the dedication of the Riddle House in the early 1980s, two unexpected guests showed up for the ceremony. Resplendent in Victorian garb, the couple added authenticity to the time period being celebrated. Many assumed that they were actors who were hired for the occasion; they were not. In fact, no one knew *who* they were. A few weeks later, century-old photos from the Riddle House were put on display. There, in sepia tones, stood the very same couple that guests had encountered during the dedication!

When the *Ghost Adventures* team spent a night locked inside the Riddle House in 2008, a medium warned the investigators that the spirit of Joseph is an evil entity that did not want them there. But that didn't stop investigator Zak Bagans from provoking the spirit. Bagans left a board at the top of the stairs and asked the entity to move it if it didn't want them there. Later, after the team heard footsteps in the room above them, the board fell down several stairs on its own. Throughout the course of the night, the team experienced unexplained noises and objects moving and falling by themselves. In the end, the researchers concluded that the Riddle House is definitely haunted and that whatever resides in the attic does not like men in particular, just as the medium had cautioned.

Ethereal stirrings at the Riddle House continue to this day. Unexplained sightings of a torso hanging in the attic window represent only part of the horror. And if history is any indicator, more supernatural sightings and activity are certainly to come.

ST. AUGUSTINE: WHERE PAST AND PRESENT MEET

Founded in 1565, St. Augustine, Florida, has more than 400 years of history under its belt. As "The Nation's Oldest City," its beautiful old cemeteries are full of people who called St. Augustine home—but some of them don't seem to realize that they're dead.

OUR LADY OF LA LECHE CHURCH

America's very first Catholic mass was held at Our Lady of La Leche Church on September 8, 1565, and the church, grounds, and cemetery are still called "America's Most Sacred Acre." The holy site is now the final resting place of many nuns and priests, and it is believed that some of them still visit the church on a regular basis. The spirit of one particular nun is often seen wandering the mission grounds dressed in a black habit; she is frequently spotted kneeling in prayer in front of the chapel. A bit shy, she disappears if anyone gets too close.

THE APOPINAX TREE

Just outside Tolomato Cemetery, a ghost lingers near the famous Apopinax Tree. According to local lore, Colonel Joseph Smith met and fell in love with a married woman in 1823. After she became ill and died, her husband made plans to bury her according to the custom of the times, which included carrying her to Tolomato Cemetery in a seated position. But when the thorny branches of the Apopinax Tree scratched her face as she passed beneath, she began to bleed! Her husband tried to bury her anyway, but the Colonel insisted that she be removed from her grave. She went on to live another six years, and after her actual death, her husband commanded pallbearers to avoid the tree so that the same thing wouldn't happen again. Dressed in black, the woman still wanders throughout Tolomato Cemetery, apparently looking for someone. Is it her husband...or her admirer?

HARRY'S SEAFOOD BAR AND GRILLE

Beware the restrooms on the second floor at Harry's Seafood Bar and Grille: They may contain an uninvited visitor. The de Porras family once owned the building, and their daughter Catalina loved it very much. Her family moved away from St. Augustine in the 1760s, but Catalina eventually returned, and she and her husband purchased the house in 1789. Unfortunately, she died soon after.

A fire destroyed the original building in 1887, but Catalina's spirit is thought to haunt the replica of her beloved home, which was built in 1888. A spectral woman wearing a white dress or nightgown is often seen near the ladies room, but no one knows for sure if it's Catalina or a female guest who perished in the fire.

SPANISH MILITARY HOSPITAL

Many spirits are thought to haunt the former Spanish Military Hospital, which is now a museum. The reconstructed building showcases rooms of the past, such as a mourning room with priests' tools for administering Last Rites; a surgeon's room with medical instruments from the 18th century; a ward, where a typical patient would have slept; and an apothecary, which stocked common medicines of the day. A host of ghosts from the old hospital are also present. Doors in the building open and close on their own, and on numerous occasions, the front door has mysteriously been unlocked with no human help. Unseen hands have touched visitors, and some people have even been scratched or bitten by malevolent entities. Footsteps are commonly heard when no one is around, strange smells linger, and objects move all by themselves—and have even been thrown at unsuspecting guests. Full-bodied apparitions of former patients have also been reported both inside and outside of the building.

ST. FRANCIS INN

Ghost hunters will want to visit Lily's Room at the St. Francis Inn—one of the oldest continuously operating hotels in the United States. Built in 1791 as a single-family home, it was converted to an inn in 1845. In those times, social classes were strictly maintained, so when the homeowner's nephew fell in love with a servant girl from Barbados, the relationship was doomed from the start. The two met secretly until the young man's uncle discovered the affair. After that, the servant girl was fired and the lovers were forbidden to see each other again. Distraught, the young man hung himself in the attic, which is now known as Lily's Room. Guests who have stayed in the room have seen the ghost of a young woman carrying sheets or towels and searching for her lover. She has also made her presence known by moving toiletries and turning lights and faucets on and off.

THE OLD JAIL

You'd think that anyone in the clink would be thrilled to escape, but that doesn't seem to be the case at St. Augustine's Old Jail—several ghosts still call it home. In the late 1800s, conditions were harsh for prisoners there. Sheriff Charles Perry was cruel, and he carried out death sentences with a vengeance. Many people lost their lives there—either as punishment (for crimes that they may or may not have committed) or due to sickness or poor sanitary conditions. Now listed on the National Register of Historic Places, the Old Jail tells its tales of the past with the spirits that linger there. Visitors hear footsteps and the sound of dragging chains mixed with the soft strains of "Swing Low, Sweet Chariot." Disembodied barking is heard quite often; it is believed to come from the phantom hounds of Sheriff Perry. Shouts and wails also pervade the corridors. And try as they might, employees can't get rid of the sweet smell of molasses that fills the air.

SPIRITS LIVE ON AT THE WEST VIRGINIA PENITENTIARY

The fact that all of West Virginia's executions used to take place at the West Virginia Penitentiary is only one of the reasons why this prison has more than its fair share of ghosts. Torture, violence, murder, and suicide were all common occurrences during its 119 years in operation, so it's no wonder that some of the people who lived there still roam its dank, dark halls.

THE HISTORY, THE PLACE

With the Gothic look of a spooky storybook castle, the West Virginia Penitentiary in Moundsville was built in the late 1800s. It was originally designed to house 480 inmates, but its population grew from 250 prisoners when it opened in 1876 to 2,400 in the early 1930s. With as many as three men sharing one tiny five-foot-by-seven-foot cell, living conditions there were atrocious.

BEATEN SPIRITS

Wardens at the West Virginia Penitentiary—which was once listed by the Department of Justice as one of the Top Ten Most Violent Correctional Facilities in the nation—issued severe punishments for those inmates who misbehaved: Prisoners were tortured, whipped, and beaten. One spirit that lingers there is believed to be that of Robert, an inmate who was beaten to death.

Over the years, many deaths occurred within the prison's walls. Some were brought on by violent treatment, poor living conditions, and illness; additionally, a total of 94 men were executed there: 85 by hanging and 9 via the electric chair. One execution began with a mishap when a man who had been sentenced to hang fell through the floor before the noose could be fixed around his neck; he had to be picked up and taken back upstairs, where he was then hung successfully. It is said that his spirit still wanders around the gallows where he died.

As early as the 1930s, folks at the prison began seeing ghosts and reporting an eerie feeling that an invisible entity was standing close by. One specter that is often seen is that of a tattletale maintenance man who spied on the inmates and liked to get them in trouble. He met his end when a group of prisoners attacked him in a bathroom, which is where his earthbound spirit remains today.

Ghostly activity has also been observed in the shower area, in the chapel, along death row, and at the execution site. And don't forget the front gate, where the turnstiles move by themselves—perhaps admitting a "new" batch of inmates. One frightening spirit at the West Virginia Pen is that of the "shadow man," whose misty shape has been spotted lurking in the dark, giving off a menacing feeling to those who see him. In fact, many of the spirits there are intimidating; they often leave people with a sense that they are being watched or even followed.

UNRULY SPIRITS

One area of the prison that investigators have found to be teeming with paranormal activity is known as "the Sugar Shack"—an area where inmates went to exercise. Although there is no official record of a death occurring there, many people have felt cold spots and heard unexplained noises, such as screams and arguing voices. Some visitors have even felt unseen hands poking them in the back or stroking them on the cheek.

If you like ghosts or history—or both—the West Virginia Pen is well worth the trip. But beware of this group of spirits: They were unhappy in life and are still unhappy in death. So if you feel the touch of something that you can't see, it might be a good idea to run.

GHOSTS OF HARPERS FERRY

Harpers Ferry, West Virginia, is a picturesque town that has been at the center of a great deal of American history, most notably during the mid-19th century, when abolitionist John Brown staged a raid that proved to be a catalyst for the American Civil War. However, Harpers Ferry is also known for its ghosts. Here are a few of the many spirits that haunt this historic town:

RACHAEL HARPER

In the mid-18th century, Robert Harper founded the town of Harpers Ferry. After he and his wife Rachael lost their first house in a flood, Harper began construction of a much grander home. But this was during the American Revolution, when laborers were hard to find, so the aging Harper did much of the work himself. He was quite concerned about lawlessness during this uncertain time, so legend has it that he instructed Rachael to bury their gold in a secret location and tell no one about it. Harper passed away in 1782, and after Rachael died unexpectedly following a fall from a ladder, the secret location of their gold was buried with her.

For many years, the Harper House has been considered haunted. People who pass it swear that they see a woman in old-fashioned clothes staring out from an upstairs window. Perhaps it's Rachael, remaining watchful and vigilant over the family's gold.

18TH-CENTURY SOLDIERS

In the waning years of the 18th century, an army was sent to Harpers Ferry in preparation for a possible war between the United States and France. The army wound up waiting for a conflict that never happened, so to relieve their boredom, the soldiers paraded to fife and drum music. Unfortunately, a cholera epidemic struck the army while it sat idle, and many men died. Today, the spirits of the men seem to remain. Almost everyone in town has heard the faint sounds of feet marching, drums beating, and fifes playing as an invisible phantom army sweeps through town, doomed to repeat its nightly musical ritual for eternity.

JOHN BROWN

John Brown is probably the most noteworthy figure associated with the town of Harpers Ferry. Many people are familiar with his tall, gaunt, white-bearded image, so perhaps it's not surprising that many have seen someone looking exactly like him wandering around town. The resemblance to Brown is so uncanny that tourists have taken photos with the spirit; however, when the pictures are developed, "Brown" is not in them. John Brown's ghost has also been spotted several miles outside of town at the Kennedy Farmhouse. It was there that Brown and his men stayed for several months while planning the raid. Even today, phantom footsteps, disembodied male voices, and snoring can be heard coming from the empty attic where the conspirators once stayed. It's no wonder that particular area of the house is largely shunned.

DANGERFIELD NEWBY

Another ghost seen at Harpers Ferry is that of Dangerfield Newby, a former slave who joined Brown's raid out of desperation after a cruel slave owner stymied his attempts to free his wife and child. Newby was the first of Brown's band to die in the raid; he was struck in the throat by a jagged spike. Vengeful townspeople mutilated his body and left it in an alley for wild hogs to devour.

Dressed in old clothes and a slouch hat, Newby's specter continues to roam the streets of Harpers Ferry, perhaps still trying to save his family or take revenge on those who treated his corpse so badly. Across his neck is a horrific scar from the spike that killed him.

THE HUNDRED DAYS' MEN

Like many other ghosts, the spirits of the Hundred Days' Men were born out of the violence of war. In 1864, at the height of the Civil War, the governor of Ohio proposed a plan that called for several northern states to enlist large numbers of men for a short period of 100 days. One such group was sent to Harpers Ferry, where they camped at Maryland Heights. One wet day, the inexperienced troops sought dry ground on which to build a fire and cook their dinner. Unfortunately, someone decided to stack some artillery shells to make a dry surface on which to place wood and vegetation. Soon a roaring fire was under way—atop the artillery shells! Inevitably, the shells exploded and many of the Hundred Days' Men were killed. Mysterious fires are sometimes reported at Maryland Heights, but locals believe that it's just the Hundred Days'

Men, still trying to eat a meal that they began more than a century ago.

ST. PETER'S CATHOLIC CHURCH

During the Civil War, St. Peter's Catholic Church was used as a hospital for wounded soldiers. One day, a wounded young soldier was brought into the churchyard and left lying on the ground as others with more severe injuries were tended to. Hours passed, and the young man's condition worsened as he slowly bled to death. By the time doctors got to him, it was too late. As he was carried into the church, he whispered weakly, "Thank God I'm saved." Then he died.

Over the years, many people have seen a bright light on the church's threshold and heard faint whispers say, "Thank God I'm saved." Some have also watched as an elderly priest emerges from the church's rectory; he turns and walks into the church—right through the wall where the front facade once stood.

JENNY THE VAGRANT

Another ghost of Harpers Ferry is that of a poor girl named Jenny, who lived in an old storage shed that had been abandoned after the railroad came to Harpers Ferry in the early 1830s. One night, Jenny's dress was set ablaze when she ventured too close to the fire she was using to heat the shed. Jenny bolted out of the shed screaming in a blind panic. Unfortunately, she ran straight onto the railroad tracks and was hit by a train. Since then, engineers have reported hearing unearthly screams for help and seeing a ball of light careening wildly down the train tracks. Frantically, they blow their whistles, but it's too late: Each engineer feels a bump as if his train has struck something, but when he goes to investigate, he finds nothing.

HAVE A GHOSTLY GOOD TIME AT THE CAROLINA INN

Built in 1924, on the campus of the University of North Carolina in Chapel Hill, the Carolina Inn was designed to be a warm and welcoming meeting place for visitors, students, and area residents alike. A perfect amalgamation of Colonial and Southern antebellum architectural styles, this 185-room inn is on the National Register of Historic Places—and it's also one of America's Top Ten Haunted Hotels.

SOME SPIRITED FUN

Some spirits find it hard to leave the places they called home in life. Such is the case with Dr. William Jacocks, a well-known physician who lived at the Carolina Inn for the last 17 years of his life. He was described as friendly and kind, but he did enjoy a good practical joke. And it seems that hasn't changed—even though he died in 1965.

Dr. Jacocks lived in Room 252, and he is still quite protective of the space: He frequently manipulates the locks to keep out potential guests. On one occasion, a maintenance worker had to climb a ladder and crawl through a window to gain entry; another time, the door had to be removed from its hinges.

If Dr. Jacocks decides to let people enter Room 252, he tries to have his fun in other ways. Two hotel guests reported waking up to the strong scent of flowers; a quick look around the room revealed that a bath mat had been rumpled and the curtains had been pulled back in a jumbled manner. On another occasion, a couple staying in the room heard a loud whoosh of air that didn't come from the heating and air-conditioning unit.

THE GHOST HUNT

By the early 2000s, the reports of inexplicable occurrences at the Carolina Inn had piqued the interest of professional ghost hunters. During one investigation, a team from a local paranormal research group set up audio recorders, digital cameras, infrared video cameras, and electromagnetic sensors. They monitored three rooms, including Room 252, for a four-hour period. And they weren't disappointed.

The investigators recorded footsteps, a door slamming, and a loud bang—all in an empty room. During one 20-minute period, they sensed the strong presence of something else in the room and even felt breath on the backs of their necks. Photos taken during this time show orbs of light, as though something was moving through the room. The sound of music playing from a distance was also heard and captured on a recording. Careful listening revealed that the music was coming from a piano, but no piano was in that room or anywhere nearby. A low murmur of voices was also audible.

BOTTOMS UP!

When the ghost hunters returned to the Carolina Inn in 2009, they heard the sound of ice cubes clinking into a glass and got the distinct feeling that they were in the presence of the spirit of a heavy drinker (which Dr. Jacocks was not). Other team members got the same impression elsewhere in the building that same night.

It seems that the good doctor may have some ghostly company. Some hotel guests have reported seeing the apparition of a large man in a black suit and winter coat wandering the halls and jiggling doorknobs before quickly disappearing.

JUST A LITTLE FUN

Several sessions of "Ghost Hunter University"—an event organized by the Carolina Inn to play up its supernatural activity—have taken place at the hotel. These events attract participants who are interested in the paranormal or like ghost stories, and they include tours and seminars about various haunted locations throughout the building.

When Christopher Moon, editor of *Haunted Times* magazine, arrived to host a session of Ghost Hunter University, he, of course, requested to stay in Room 252. And it lived up to its reputation. Photos that he took showed orbs in the room, which are said to indicate a paranormal presence. But the best evidence of ghost play?

When he went to use the bathroom sink, both handles fell right off and into the basin, spraying water everywhere. Somewhere, Dr. Jacocks was having a good laugh.

NORTH CAROLINA'S TRAIN OF TERROR

North Carolina is rife with haunted houses. In fact, even the Governor's Mansion in Raleigh is said to contain a ghost or two. But one of the Tarheel State's most unusual paranormal events isn't housebound—it takes place on an isolated train trestle known as the Bostian Bridge near the town of Statesville.

THE HISTORY

On August 27, 1891, a passenger train jumped the tracks while crossing the Bostian Bridge, plunging seven railcars 60 to 75 feet to the ground below. Nearly 30 people perished in the tragic accident. According to local legend, on the anniversary of the catastrophe, the sounds of screeching wheels, screaming passengers, and a thunderous crash can be heard near the Bostian Bridge. The specter of a uniformed man carrying a gold pocket watch has also been observed lingering nearby.

ANOTHER VICTIM CLAIMED

Sadly, on August 27, 2010, Christopher Kaiser, a Charlotte-based amateur ghost hunter, was struck and killed by a real-life train that surprised him on the Bostian Bridge. According to police reports, Kaiser had brought a small group to the trestle in hopes of experiencing the eerie sounds that are said to occur on the anniversary of the 1891 crash. The group was standing on the span when a Norfolk-Southern train turned a corner and headed toward them. With the train rapidly approaching, Kaiser managed to push the woman in front of him off the tracks. His heroic action saved her life but cost him his own.

Other than witnessing this horrific accident, Kaiser's group saw nothing unusual that night. But many others claim to have seen strange phenomena on the Bostian Bridge. On the 50th anniversary of the 1891 tragedy, for example, one woman reportedly watched the wreck occur all over again. More than 150 people gathered near the trestle on the 100th anniversary of the crash in 1991, but nothing supernatural happened that night.

GUEST GHOSTS ARE THE NORM AT AUSTIN'S DRISKILL HOTEL

Southern hospitality abounds at the Driskill Hotel in downtown Austin, Texas. Built in 1886 by local cattle baron Colonel Jesse Lincoln Driskill, this lodging is hardly short on amenities. As a member of Historic Hotels of America and Associated Luxury Hotels International, the Driskill offers every comfort imaginable: From fancy linens and plasma-screen TVs to fine dining and complimentary shoeshines, this Austin institution has it all—including a few resident ghosts.

Since it opened, the Driskill has been a magnet for the rich and famous: Lyndon and Lady Bird Johnson had their first date at the hotel's restaurant, and Amelia Earhart, Louis Armstrong, and Richard Nixon have all sought respite there. At the Driskill, the upscale clientele mixes with the invisible guests that reside there full-time—the true spirits of the hotel.

MEET THE GHOSTS

Considered one of the most haunted hotels in the United States, the Driskill is the eternal home of many spirits. First and foremost would have to be the ghost of Colonel Driskill himself. He makes his presence known by entering random guest rooms and smoking the cigars that he once loved so dearly. Driskill is also said to play with the lights in bathrooms, turning them on and off for fun.

Hotel guests and employees have seen water faucets turn on and off by themselves; some have even reported hearing the sound of noisy guests coming from an empty elevator. Others have felt as if they were being pushed out of bed, and some wake in the morning to find that their room's furniture has been rearranged during the night.

A GHOST WITH FASHION SENSE

When singer Annie Lennox stayed at the Driskill Hotel in the 1980s while performing in Austin, she laid out two dresses to consider after she got out of the shower. When she emerged from the bathroom, only one dress was still on the bed; the other was once again hanging in the closet.

A ghost dressed in Victorian-era clothing has been seen at night where the front desk used to stand, and guests have detected the scent of roses in the area. This is believed to be the spirit of Mrs. Bridges, who worked at the Driskill as a front-desk clerk in the early 1900s.

The spirit of a young girl haunts the lobby on the first floor; she is believed to have been the daughter of a senator. In 1887, she was chasing a ball on the grand staircase when she tripped and fell to her death. Today, her ghost is often heard laughing and bouncing a ball up and down those same stairs.

The spirit of Peter J. Lawless might still be residing in Room 419, where he lived from 1886 until 1916 or 1917. Although the housekeeping crew cleans and vacuums that room like all the others, they often report finding rumpled bedclothes, open dresser drawers, and footprints in the bathroom—after they've already cleaned the room. Lawless is typically blamed for this mischievous behavior, and his specter is also often spotted near the elevators on the fifth floor. He pauses to check his watch when the doors open—then he promptly disappears.

IN THE SPIRIT OF THINGS

A more modern ghost that hangs around the Driskill is the "Houston Bride." When her fiancé called off their wedding plans in the 1990s, the young woman did what many other jilted brides would be tempted to do: She stole his credit cards and went shopping! She was last seen on the hotel elevator, loaded down with her packages. Retail therapy was apparently not the cure, however: She was found dead a few days later, the victim of a gunshot wound to the abdomen. Some guests have seen her apparition with her arms full of packages; others have spotted her in her wedding gown. Oddly, it seems to be those guests who are at the hotel for weddings or bachelorette parties that are most likely to see her. And even stranger, some brides consider it good luck to catch a glimpse of the tragic "Houston Bride" before their own weddings. Maybe she counts as "something blue."

CATFISH PLANTATION

Fort Worth Paranormal once deemed the Catfish Plantation in Waxahachie, Texas, "one of the most haunted restaurants in the entire country," and with several earthbound spirits in residence there, this quaint Victorian building lives up to that designation.

THE PARANORMAL PROGNOSIS

As is the case at many haunted places, this restaurant has cold spots, doors that lock and unlock by themselves, water faucets and lights that turn on and off without human intervention, and refrigerator doors that open and close on their own. In addition, a number of dinner knives mysteriously come up missing every night. Perhaps some of this is the doing of the restaurant's three resident ghosts. The quietest spirit is that of Will, a farmer who died of pneumonia when he lived in the building in the 1930s; he's been seen loitering on the front porch. It is believed that he is responsible for some of the cold spots. He's typically very shy, but he has been known to touch women's legs while they're eating.

A more active ghost is that of Elizabeth Anderson, a young woman who lived in the building until the early 1920s, when a former boyfriend murdered her on the day that she was supposed to marry another man. Her appearances are preceded by the scent of roses. Elizabeth is sometimes seen in the bay window in the front room. Once, she even followed a customer home and presented her with an antique powder box as a gift.

A third spirit that resides at the Catfish Plantation is believed to be that of a woman named Caroline, who died in the building in the 1970s at age 80. Although no one has actually seen her ghost, her presence is deeply felt, and she wants to remind everyone that the building is still her home. When the restaurant opened in 1984, Caroline greeted the new owner with a pot of freshly brewed coffee. Another time, the owner was surprised to discover a large tea urn positioned in the middle of the kitchen floor; all the cups were stacked neatly inside it. Caroline has also been known to throw coffee cups, wineglasses, spices, and food.

FORT WORTH STOCKYARDS

The spirits haunting the Fort Worth Stockyards are well aware they are in Texas, because they have made their hauntings as prominent as possible—exactly as state custom requires!

WHAT, ALL HAT AND NO CATTLE?

Well, the Stockyards used to have quite a few head of beef, but now they mostly have tourists. Today the Fort Worth Stockyards are a historic district (or a tourist trap, depending on perspective) like Vancouver's Gastown or Wichita's Cowtown. Fort Worthians revel in the ghosty spice that seasons the Stockyards' history. For a slight fee, some will take you on a tour. Here are some of the highlights.

GOOD GOLLY...

One of the Stockyards' most famous haunted spots is Miss Molly's Hotel, formerly a boardinghouse, speakeasy and bordello. Seven themed and named rooms are lush with all the all the attendant décor you'd expect. The Cattleman's and Cowboy's rooms are notorious for ghost sightings. Most commonly, the apparitions look like young women, perhaps the spirits of past 'soiled doves' who too often came to grief in the old West. One modern housekeeper quit after extra coins kept appearing after she'd already collected her tips!

CANTINA CADILLAC

This hopping night spot is so haunted that at night, it always has at least two staffers. Tills are often short or over, with the shortage or overage made up the next day. This could just be human error, except that it happens here suspiciously more often than in most establishments. One day, while closing out downstairs, the Cantina crew heard noise topside. They went up to find all the furniture shoved into the middle of the dance floor. Clever prank or ghost? We don't know.

CATTLEMEN'S STEAKHOUSE

Would you like some spirits with your enormous medium rare rib eye? Can do, if you can get staff to take you downstairs at the Cattlemen's—they go in pairs. Disembodied voices call their names, doors open and close unattended, and stuff gets moved around at random. Ghost hunters have bagged some nice orb photos here, and an actual ghost photo adorns the upstairs wall—an odd face behind a bolo-hat-wearing mortal.

MAVERICK BUILDING

It has seen many uses, including its current incarnation as a western apparel store. Of old, the Maverick was a saloon, and reputedly Bonnie Parker's (as in Bonnie and Clyde) favorite gambling joint. The ghost upstairs is believed to be female, probably hailing from the brothel days of the early 20th century. Even when the Stockyards mostly smelled of cattle, and what goes into and comes out of them, one could smell roses upstairs. Years back, someone experimented by leaving a bouquet of roses upstairs. She came back later to find them tastefully distributed throughout the rooms.

WHITE ELEPHANT SALOON

In the old days, this was one of the rougher and sleazier drunkeries, and was in a different location. When that old structure crumbled, owners moved all the memorabilia here with the name. It seems that the unseen inhabitants came along, or were perhaps already in residence. Three violent deaths have occurred in the basement of the current building, leaving it with a creepy sensation. As with many hauntings, the staff describe glasses and implements mysteriously moving to new locations.

KNIFE ALLEY...

...is an alley no more, since people roofed and walled it. Today you can buy some of the finest blades in Texas in this shop. You can also watch the power go out, which the local utility finds very suspicious, considering that they have replaced the transformer three times. Ghost hunters reckon that paranormal activity might be to blame, since all mundane explanations have been ruled out.

OTHER SIGHTINGS IN THE AREA

- **Arnaud's (New Orleans, Louisiana)**

The ghost of a man dressed in an old-fashioned tuxedo is often spotted near the windows of the main dining room. But this ghost, believed to be that of Arnaud Cazenave, the first owner of the establishment, is not alone. A ghostly woman has been seen walking out of the restroom and moving silently across the restaurant before disappearing into a wall.

- **Poogan's Porch (Charleston, South Carolina)**

Originally built as a house in 1888, the building underwent major renovations and reopened as a restaurant in 1976. Perhaps it was those renovations that brought the ghost of Zoe St. Amand, former owner of the house, back to see what all the fuss was about. Zoe's ghost is described as an older woman in a long black dress who silently wanders through the establishment at all hours of the day and night.

- ## Sally's Bridge (Concord, North Carolina)

Just outside of Concord is a bridge on Poplar Tent Road that locals refer to as Sally's Bridge. According to local lore, a young woman named Sally was driving home with her baby when she lost control of her car, skidded across the bridge, and crashed. The baby was ejected from the vehicle and fell into the water. Panic-stricken, Sally dove into the water to try to save her child, but sadly both mother and child drowned. Today, legend has it that Sally's ghost will bang on your car, desperately trying to find someone to help save her dying child.

- ## Blennerhassett Hotel (Parkersburg, West Virginia)

The Blennerhassett Hotel was designed and built in 1889 by William Chancellor, a prominent businessman. The hotel was a grand showplace and has been restored to its original condition in recent years. These renovations have reportedly stirred the ghosts who reside there into action.

There are several ghosts associated with the hotel, including a man in gray who has been seen walking around on the second floor and the infamous "Four O'Clock Knocker," who likes to pound on guest room doors at 4:00 A.M. There is also a ghost who likes to ride the elevators, often stopping on floors where the button has not been pushed. But the most famous resident spirit is that of hotel builder William Chancellor. Guests and employees have reported seeing clouds of cigar smoke in the hallways, wafting through doorways, and circling a portrait of Chancellor that hangs in the library.

CHAPTER 5

THE WEST

THE GHOSTS OF SEATTLE'S PIKE PLACE MARKET

Pike Place Market, which opened in August 1907, is one of the oldest farmers' markets in the United States. On its first day in business, more than 10,000 shoppers besieged the eight farmers who had brought their wares to Seattle's waterfront. By year's end, the market's first building was open, and it hasn't looked back since. Perhaps that's a good thing, because looking back might well reveal something else besides shoppers: ghosts.

One of the market's most frequent phantom visitors is Princess Angeline, the daughter of Chief Seattle, who was a leader of the tribes that lived in the area before the arrival of white settlers. By the late 1850s, many Native Americans had left the area due to the terms of a treaty between the tribes and the U.S. government. But Angeline stayed in Seattle and was a familiar figure along the waterfront. She became a local celebrity and was frequently photographed later in life.

Angeline died in 1896 at age 85. So when Pike Place Market was built on the site of her former home, it was like sending out an open invitation for her to hang around for a while, and Angeline has apparently accepted the offer. Her apparition has been spotted at many different locations in the market, but she seems particularly fond of a wooden column on the lower level. Abnormally cold air is said to surround this column, and photographs of it reputedly show things that aren't apparent to the naked eye.

With her braided gray hair, slow way of moving, and habit of browsing, Angeline's ghost easily passes for an elderly shopper. She has often fooled people, who react to her as if she's a fellow consumer until she startles them by vanishing right before their eyes. Sometimes, Angeline even treats folks to a light show, changing from a glowing white figure to blue, lavender, or pink.

YOU'RE NEVER ALONE AT PIKE PLACE MARKET

While Angeline does her best to make as many ghostly appearances at the market as possible, she's not the only spectral spectacle at Pike Place. Workers have heard disembodied lullabies drifting through the air late at night after the market is closed; allegedly, they come from the ghost of a heavyset female barber who used to softly sing her customers to sleep and then pick their pockets while they snoozed. Unfortunately, she was not as good at walking as singing, and one day she fell through a weak floor to her death. Nevertheless, her ethereal song continues, which seems to contradict the saying, "It ain't over until the fat lady sings."

Another spirit that calls Pike Place home is Arthur Goodwin, the market's director from 1918 to 1941. Ever the workaholic, Arthur's silhouette can often be seen looking down at the market from his former office on the upper floor, still keeping an eye on the business.

What's more, a small spectral boy is seen in a craft shop that sells beads. He's been known to open and shut the cash register and tug at sleeves to get attention. At one point during renovations to the store, a small cache of beads was discovered in a wall; it's believed that the ghostly boy was stashing beads there to play with later, as kids often do.

A SPECTER WITH A SWEET TOOTH

Some more temperamental ghosts have been heard arguing inside the walk-in freezer of a Pike Place deli. A few deli employees simply refuse to go into the freezer because they're afraid of being drawn into whatever disagreement these spirits have with each other.

Other ghostly goings-on occur in a bookshop, where employees—who swear that they're the only ones in the store—sometimes hear footsteps echoing through the aisles. And proving that even a ghost can have a sweet tooth, a candy store at the market has its own resident ghost. On several occasions, employees have put the candy scoops away at night, only to find them back out the next morning.

The next time you're in Seattle, be sure to visit Pike Place Market, and remember that the person standing next to you might just be a visitor from the Other Side.

OLD MONTANA PRISON INMATES SERVE LIFE SENTENCES

In 1871, the Old Montana Prison opened its gates in Deer Lodge after citizens of the territory realized that laws needed to be enforced and the wilder elements of the region needed to be punished. Like many other prisons of the day, this facility soon became overcrowded, which led to sickness, poor living conditions, prisoner unrest, and the taut emotions that lead to restless spirits and residual hauntings.

NO ESCAPE

The year 1890 marked the beginning of the Conley era—a time when prison warden Frank Conley ruled with an iron fist and put his prisoners to work. But Conley also made significant improvements to both the prison itself and the lives of the inmates. He even established camps that sent the prisoners outside to work in the community.

However, this outside work was a privilege, and in 1908, two prisoners who were not allowed this freedom decided to take matters into their own hands. Their attempted escape resulted in the murder of the deputy prison warden and 103 stitches in the back and neck of Warden Conley. The two would-be escapees were hanged in the prison yard for their crime.

After that, the prison underwent many changes, including the end of prisoners working outside the facility, the addition of a women's prison, and the creation of a license plate manufacturing plant.

In 1959, the Old Montana Prison experienced a riot that lasted for three days and nights. Several inmates attempted to escape by holding the warden hostage and killing the deputy warden on the spot. After the National Guard was called in to end the melee, the two ringleaders died in a murder/suicide.

THE MAIN ATTRACTION

The Old Montana Prison closed for good in 1979, and a year later, the building opened its doors to the public as a museum. In addition to offering historical tours, the museum also offers tours for those who are interested in things that go bump in the night. In fact, so much paranormal activity has been experienced at the Old Montana Prison that several ghost-hunting television shows have traveled there to investigate and film episodes.

In 2010, a *Ghost Lab* episode titled "No Escape" depicted Brad and Barry Klinge's (founders of Everyday Paranormal) visit to the prison. A wealth of high-tech ghost-hunting equipment helped the investigators uncover supernatural phenomena ranging from mysterious whispers and the sound of footsteps in empty rooms and hallways to objects flying through the air. The investigators also experienced a general feeling of dread and the unshakeable sensation that they were being watched.

SEE FOR YOURSELF

While touring the old prison, one can almost imagine
the place as it was in the old days. Many people report
hearing the shuffling of cards in the cellblocks, as well as
mumbled voices and footsteps. Arguments have even been
known to break out between people who aren't visible.

Shadows and ghostly figures are common sights at the
museum, and some visitors have reported seeing objects
flying through the air in violent, threatening ways.
People have also experienced a myriad of emotions and
sensations: Some have reported feeling deep sadness or
dread overtake them. And even more frightening, others
have perceived that someone or something is choking or
attacking them.

LIVING WITH THE GHOSTS

Museum Director Julia Brewer is rather matter-of-fact about
the hauntings in the old prison. After all, she has smelled
burning flesh in her office for the better part of a decade,
so you could say that she's a believer.

Brewer leads many of the groups that tour the facility,
so she knows most of the prison lore. She also knows how
to treat the spirits, and cautions visitors to treat the dead
with respect...or else face the consequences.

A place known as the Death Tower produces a high level
of otherworldly energy—it's where inmates Jerry Myles and
Lee Smart died in a murder/suicide during the 1959 riot.
A place called the Steam Hole carries some heavy energy

of its own. Prisoners who were deemed unruly were often sent there; at least one prisoner died in the Steam Hole under suspicious circumstances, and another inmate took his own life there by hanging himself from a pipe.

Several ghosts are known to haunt the prison grounds, and many visitors—especially psychics and ghost hunters who are sensitive to the spirit world—have experienced odd and sinister sensations. Some have even reported feeling physically ill.

PLAYFUL SPIRITS

A couple of ghosts are even known to hang around the museum's gift shop. One is the spirit of an inmate named Calvin, who was beaten to death in a corner of the room when it was an industrial area of the prison. Now the site houses a shelf of dolls, perhaps to neutralize the violence. A spirit that the staff refers to as "Stinker" also frequents the gift shop. The jokester of the pair, he likes to play pranks, such as moving merchandise around.

You'd think that ghosts would stick to their old haunts within the prison, but another place on the grounds that definitely seems haunted is the Montana Auto Museum, which is located just outside the gift shop. Staffers and visitors have seen ghostly figures there, and people have heard car doors slam when no one else is around.

And then there's the spirit of a young girl that has been observed by visitors at the auto museum. When a group reached the building on one ghost tour, the leader invited any spirits to show themselves by turning on a flashlight;

the playful ghost did. The group also asked her to move a chain that was cordoning off the cars; she did that too.

In a place that's harbored more than its share of violence and despair, the ghost of a little girl seems pretty benign. But as tour guides warn groups about the spirits of the Old Montana Prison: Be careful...they might just follow you home.

A HOST OF GHOSTS HAUNT THE WHITE EAGLE SALOON

The building housing the White Eagle Saloon in Portland, Oregon, has been many things since it was constructed in the early 1900s: a hotel, a brothel, a rooming house, and, most recently, a tavern that features live music. For much of its history, it has also been haunted.

Over the years, a great deal of paranormal activity has been reported at the White Eagle Saloon. Most of it has been harmless—but not all of it. For example, many years ago, a waitress was walking to the basement after closing to tabulate the day's receipts when something unseen shoved her down the stairs. The woman's hysterical screams got the attention of the bartender and doorman, who had a bucket hurled at them by an invisible force. Not surprisingly, the waitress quit the next day.

To date, this is the most violent outburst from the spirits at the White Eagle Saloon; however, many other, more innocuous events that simply defy explanation have occurred there.

WEIRDNESS IN THE BATHROOM

One of the White Eagle's ghosts seems to enjoy flushing the toilet in the men's room. Many people have observed this unusual activity, usually after closing. A faulty toilet? No way, says owner Chuck Hughes—the flushing has occurred with two different commodes, and it is sometimes accompanied by the sound of footsteps in the hallway outside the restroom.

Hughes has experienced quite a bit of unexplained phenomena over the years. For example, one day he was removing a lock from a door on the second floor when he heard what sounded like a woman crying at the other end of the hallway. But as he walked toward the source of the noise, the crying ceased. Hughes checked all of the rooms on the second floor but found nothing. When he returned to his work on the door, the crying began again. Hughes again tried to find the source of the sound, and this time, he felt an overwhelming chill.

Frightened, Hughes rushed downstairs and exited the tavern. Looking back at the building, he saw what he later described as a ghostly shape in one of the second-floor windows. After moving to the back of the building, Hughes saw the same specter at another window. Shaken, he refused to go upstairs again for nearly a year.

A GHOST NAMED SAM

It is believed that one of the ghosts haunting the White Eagle Saloon is a former employee named Sam, who some say was adopted at a young age by one of the building's early owners. A burly guy, Sam lived and worked at the White Eagle until his death in the 1930s.

After Sam died in his room at the White Eagle, his boss had his body removed and then locked the room and left it pretty much the way it was for a long time. Is Sam still hanging around the tavern? Many believe so. Hughes recalled that after he bought the White Eagle, the door to Sam's room would not stay open. Time after time, the door was left open, only to be found shut—and locked—a couple of days later. Apparently, Sam likes his privacy.

Hughes says that he's experienced enough unexplained phenomena at the White Eagle to fill a book. For example, he used to keep a bed in the basement to use when he worked late; one night, he awoke to find himself being nudged by invisible hands. Understandably disconcerted, he got dressed and went home.

While working in the basement after hours, Hughes often heard voices and footsteps above him; sometimes the voices even called his name. But every time he went to investigate, no one was there.

SUSPECTED SPOOKS

The White Eagle Saloon has hosted its share of wild times and even wilder characters over the years, so it's no surprise that it's haunted. Sam is believed to be the spook that flushes the men's room toilet, and the crying woman may be the spirit of one of the many prostitutes who worked there when the building housed a brothel.

But who pushed the waitress down the cellar stairs? Some suspect that it was the ghost of a Chinese bouncer known for harshly treating the African American prostitutes who worked in the basement. One day, the guy simply disappeared. Was he murdered? If so, it might explain why his angry spirit is still attached to the White Eagle.

SPIRITS SHINE ON AT THE STANLEY HOTEL

The Stanley Hotel—a beautiful Georgian-style resort in Estes Park, Colorado—was the inspiration for the Overlook Hotel in Stephen King's famous novel The Shining *and the movie adaptation, which starred Jack Nicholson. Fortunately, unlike at King's fictional inn, the ghosts of the Stanley Hotel are not malicious. But rest assured, there are definitely ghosts at this famous hotel.*

HOW IT ALL BEGAN

In 1903, F. O. Stanley—inventor of the Stanley Steamer automobile—was suffering from tuberculosis and was told that he had just months to live. That year, Stanley and his wife, Flora, visited Estes Park hoping to find some relief in the thin mountain air. They fell in love with its majestic Rocky Mountain landscape and decided to move there permanently. Shortly thereafter, construction began on the Stanley Hotel, which was completed in 1909. (Stanley died in 1940 at the ripe old age of 91, so apparently the mountain air did the trick.)

Nestled in the mountains, the resort offers a spectacular view. Many notable guests have stayed at the Stanley Hotel, including John Philip Sousa, President Theodore Roosevelt, Japanese royalty, members of the Hollywood set—including Jim Carrey, Rebecca De Mornay, and Elliott Gould—and, of course, writer Stephen King.

FRIENDLY GHOSTS

King stayed in Room 237, which is the haunted room in *The Shining*. However, most of the paranormal activity at the Stanley seems to occur on the fourth floor, specifically in Room 418. There, guests have heard children laughing and playing, but when they complain that the children are too loud, no children are ever found.

In Room 407, a ghost likes to play with the lights. However, it's apparently a reasonable spook: When guests ask it to turn the lights back on, it does.

During his stay, Stephen King alerted the staff that a young boy on the second floor was calling for his nanny. Of course, the staff members at the Stanley were well aware of the ghostly boy, who had been spotted throughout the hotel many times over the years.

But the two most prominent spirits at the resort are those of F. O. Stanley and his wife. Flora makes her presence known by playing the piano in the ballroom. Even those who haven't seen her claim to hear piano music coming from the ballroom when it's empty, and some have seen the piano keys move up and down of their own accord.

F. O. Stanley's specter most often manifests in the lobby, the bar, and the billiard room, which were apparently his favorite spots in the building when he was alive.

A GHOSTLY VISITOR

When Jason Hawes and Grant Wilson from the television show *Ghost Hunters* stayed at the Stanley Hotel in 2006, their investigation hit paranormal pay dirt. Hawes stayed in Room 401—purportedly one of the most haunted guest rooms—and set up a video camera to record anything that occurred while he was asleep. Although the picture is dark, the camera captured the distinct sounds of a door opening and glass breaking—all while Hawes was sound asleep. When he got up to investigate, he noticed that the closet door had been opened and a glass on the nightstand was broken. Later, the camera recorded the closet door closing—and latching—with no humans in sight.

Wilson had his own paranormal experience in Room 1302: He was sitting at a table with some other team members when the table lifted off the ground and crashed back down—all of its own accord. When the group tried to raise the table, they found it to be so heavy that it took several people to lift it even a few inches.

During a follow-up session at the Stanley Hotel, those in attendance were also treated to paranormal activity. K-2 meters were used to detect changes in the electromagnetic field (which indicate that a ghost is nearby), and they lit up time and again. Clear responses to questions directed at the resident spirits were also captured on audio recordings.

MEET THE SPIRITS

The Stanley Hotel offers ghost tours to educate visitors about the paranormal activity within its walls. Or if you'd rather just stay in your room, you could always watch a movie—*The Shining* runs continuously on the guest-room televisions.

THE HAUNTING OF THE PHOENIX THEATRE

Audiences that saw A Chorus Line at the Phoenix Theatre in 2005 got a little more than they bargained for when an unpaid and uncredited dancer twirled her way between the chorus-line performers. Those who saw her may have thought it was odd that a ballerina was prancing around in a show about Broadway dancers. Of course, they may have found it even stranger if they realized that she was just one of the many ghosts that inhabit the theater, which opened in 1951.

THE HAUNTING IN THE VALLEY

Members of Arizona's Phoenix Theatre Company have been entertaining locals and visitors with a variety of productions since 1920. As the oldest arts institution in Arizona, it makes sense that a few of its ghosts want to make one last curtain call.

The aforementioned ghost—which the staff affectionately calls "Tiny Dancer"—is not the only spirit at the Phoenix Theatre with artistic inclinations. "Mr. Electrics" is the spirit of an old man who is sometimes seen sitting on the pipes that hold the lighting instruments. He also appears late at night to help the technicians by manipulating buttons. Another ghost that deals with lighting is referred to as "Light Board Lenny;" he hangs around the lighting booth and has been known to playfully lock out lightboard operators and spotlight technicians if they leave their positions in the booth. The spirit known as the "Prop Master" takes a cue from Lenny and sometimes locks people out of the prop room so that it can dig through the props.

Unfortunately, not all the spirits at the Phoenix Theatre are so lighthearted. One of the theater's ghosts is believed to be the angry spirit of Freddy, an actor who was fired from a production and then was killed while riding his bicycle home. Freddy generally likes to make a racket by slamming doors and stomping around in the theater's upstairs rooms.

With all the extra help, it's no wonder that the Phoenix Theatre Company is one of the nation's oldest continuously operating artistic troupes. Hopefully, they will be successful for years to come because ghosts hate auditioning.

TOMBSTONE SHADOWS

In its heyday, Tombstone, Arizona, was known as the town too tough to die. Apparently, its ghosts liked that moniker because there are so many spirits roaming its streets that Tombstone is a strong contender for the title of "Most Haunted Town in America." Here are a few of the most notable phantoms that still call this Wild West town home.

VIRGIL EARP

A man in a long black frock coat stands on a sidewalk in Tombstone; the people who see him assume that he's a reenactor in this former rough-and-tumble Wild West town. But as he starts across the street, a strange thing happens: He vanishes in mid-stride. Only then do people realize that they've just seen one of the many ghosts that haunt this legendary town.

It is usually assumed that the man in the black coat is the ghost of U.S. Deputy Marshal Virgil Earp, who may be reliving one of his life's darkest moments. On December 28, 1881, he was shot and wounded when outlaws who sought revenge for the infamous Gunfight at the O.K. Corral two months prior ambushed him. Virgil survived the attack, but his left arm was permanently maimed.

MORGAN EARP

In March 1882, another group of outlaws—who were also seeking revenge for the Gunfight at the O.K. Corral—gunned down Morgan Earp, the brother of noted lawmen Virgil and Wyatt Earp. Morgan was shot in the back and killed while playing pool. Some say that you can still hear his dying words whispered at the location where he was murdered.

BIG NOSE KATE

Big Nose Kate was the girlfriend of gunslinger Doc Holliday, a friend of the Earps. Her ghost is reportedly responsible for the footsteps and snatches of whispered conversation that swirl through the Crystal Palace Saloon. Lights there turn on and off by themselves, and gambling wheels sometimes spin for no reason, causing speculation that, just as in life, Kate prefers the company of rowdy men.

SWAMPER

Big Nose Kate's Saloon was originally the Grand Hotel, and a man known as Swamper used to work there as a handyman. He lived in the basement, not far from some of the town's silver mines, so when he wasn't working, Swamper dug a tunnel to one of the mines and began supplementing his income with silver nuggets.

After all the effort that he'd put into obtaining the silver, Swamper was not about to let it go easily...not even after he died. He reportedly haunts Big Nose Kate's Saloon; perhaps he's still hanging around to protect his loot, which has never been found. He's often spotted in the basement and in photos taken by visitors.

THE BIRD CAGE THEATRE

Anyplace where 26 people were violently killed is almost certain to be a spectral smorgasbord. Such is the case with Tombstone's infamously bawdy Bird Cage Theatre.

One of the most frequently seen apparitions at the Bird Cage is that of a man who carries a clipboard and wears striped pants and a card-dealer's visor. He's been known to suddenly appear on stage, glide across it, and then walk through a wall. Visitors have raved to the management about how authentic-looking the Wild West costumes look, only to be told that nobody at the Bird Cage dresses in period clothing.

One night, an employee watched on a security monitor as a vaporous woman in white walked slowly through the cellar long after closing time. And although smoking and drinking are now prohibited at the Bird Cage, the scents of cigar smoke and whiskey still linger there. Visitors also hear unexplained sounds, such as a woman singing, a female sighing, glasses clinking, and cards shuffling, as if the ghosts are trying to finish a game that's gone on for far too long.

NELLIE CASHMAN'S RESTAURANT

Nellie Cashman's is another haunted hot spot in Tombstone. Patrons at the eatery report hearing strange noises and seeing dishes suddenly crash to the floor. And the ghosts at Nellie Cashman's have no patience for skeptics: A patron who once noisily derided all things supernatural found herself suddenly wearing the contents of a mustard container that inexplicably leaped off a table.

FRED WHITE

Of the many deaths in Tombstone during the days of the Wild West, one of the most tragic was that of town marshal Fred White. In October 1880, White was trying to arrest "Curly Bill" Brocius when Brocius's gun accidentally went off, killing the lawman. White is rumored to haunt a street near where he was killed, apparently still angry with the way his life was so abruptly taken from him.

BOOTHILL GRAVEYARD

It would almost defy belief if Tombstone's legendary Boothill Graveyard wasn't haunted, but not to worry: The final resting place of so many who were violently taken from this life is said to harbor many restless spirits, including that of Billy Clanton, one of the victims of the Gunfight at the O.K. Corral. Clanton's apparition has been seen rising from his grave and walking toward town. Strange lights and sounds are also said to come from the cemetery.

GEORGE BUFORD

Violent death came in all forms in Tombstone. One of those occurred when a man named George Buford shot his lover and then himself. His aim was better the second time, though: She lived, but he died. He is said to haunt the building where he once lived, which is now a bed-and-breakfast. His spirit has been seen in and around the building; random lights appear there for no reason, and the doorbell sometimes rings on its own in the middle of the night. And ghostly George hasn't lost his fondness for the ladies: Women in the house have felt their hair being stroked and sensed light pressure on the backs of their necks. Of course, when they turn around, no one is there.

YUMA TERRITORIAL PRISON HOLDS INMATES FOR LIFE AND DEATH

What could be worse than being locked in a prison cell for life? How about being locked in a prison that you were forced to help build? That's what happened to the first seven inmates at the Yuma Territorial Prison back in 1876. Is it any wonder that the place is considered one of the most haunted locations in Arizona?

DETAINEES IN THE DUNES

There were no minimum- or maximum-security prisons in the 1800s, so inmates at the Yuma Prison ranged from petty thieves to murderers. By the time the prison closed in 1909, more than 3,000 convicts had been held within its walls. Compared to today's standards, prison life back then was hard. Each cell measured only nine feet by nine feet, and it was not uncommon for the indoor temperature to reach 110 degrees in the summer. A punishment known as the Dark Cell was similar to what we now call solitary confinement. And a ball and chain were used to punish prisoners who tried to escape. It must have worked because plenty of souls never left this place.

THE GOOD, THE BAD, AND THE GHOSTLY

Despite the brutal conditions, a library and educational programs were available to inmates, and a prison clinic even gave them access to medical care. But the jail soon became overcrowded, and in such close quarters, tuberculosis ran rampant. During its 33-year history, 111 prisoners died there, many from TB; eight were gunned down in unsuccessful escape attempts.

From 1910 to 1914, the former prison building housed Yuma High School. Considering the restless souls that were left over from the structure's days as a prison, it probably did not make for the best educational experience. During the Great Depression, homeless families sought shelter within its walls. And later, local residents who wanted to have a little piece of Arizona history "borrowed" stones from the building's walls for their personal construction projects.

SOLITARY SPIRITS

Today, all that remains of the former Yuma Territorial Prison are some cells, the main gate, a guard tower, the prison cemetery—and the ghosts. A museum is located on the site, and visitors and employees report that spirits have settled there as well. Lights turn on and off randomly; objects are moved from one place to another; and once, the coins from the gift shop's cash register leaped into the air and then fell back into place.

The Dark Cell is also a focal point for ghostly activity: The restless spirits of prisoners who were sent there for disobeying rules are thought to linger. At least two inmates were transferred directly from that cell to an insane asylum, but whether anyone actually died there is unknown. It makes for a few unsettled spirits, though, doesn't it?

Linda Offeney, an employee at the prison site, once reported feeling an unseen presence in the Dark Cell. And a tourist who visited the prison in the 1930s had her photo taken near the Dark Cell; the picture looked perfectly normal—except for the ghostly figure of a man standing behind her within the cell. Offeney also tells the story of a writer for *Arizona Highways* magazine who witnessed the hauntings: The journalist wanted to spend two days and two nights in the cell just as prisoners would have—in the dark, with only bread and water. She only made it a few hours before she called for assistance, explaining that she couldn't shake the feeling that something was in the cell with her.

In June 2005, Arizona Desert Ghost Hunters spent the night at the Yuma Territorial Prison and gathered enough evidence to convince them that the place is indeed haunted. Photos taken of the guard tower and in Cell 14 both show suspicious activity: An orb can be seen near the tower and a misty figure is clearly visible in

Cell 14, where inmate John Ryan hung himself in 1903. The investigators also captured EVPs (electronic voice phenomena) in Cell 14, where a voice said, "Get away," and in the Dark Cell, where a male spirit told the group to "Get out of here."

Although the Yuma Territorial Prison only operated for 33 years, it certainly spawned its fair share of paranormal activity. This begs the questions: Was the prison built so soundly that there was no escape for many, even in death? Or did the inmates just give up and choose to stay there forever?

STALKED BY AN INVISIBLE ENTITY

In November 1988, when Jackie Hernandez moved into a small bungalow on 11th Street in San Pedro, California, she was looking to make a fresh start. But her hopefulness quickly turned into what she described as the "nightmare of all nightmares."

From the time that Jackie moved in to her new place, she felt a presence in the house. At first, it made her feel safe— as if someone was looking out for her. But Jackie soon realized that the presence was less than friendly. Shortly after their arrival, Jackie and her young children heard a high-pitched screeching noise throughout the house. Then, in February 1989, Jackie's unseen houseguests manifested in the form of two separate apparitions: One was an old man that Jackie's friend also witnessed while she was babysitting in the home; the other was a disembodied head that Jackie saw in the attic.

CALL IN THE CAVALRY

In August 1989, Jackie asked a group of paranormal researchers to investigate the phenomena; parapsychologist Dr. Barry Taff, cameraman Barry Conrad, and photographer Jeff Wheatcraft had no idea how the case would impact their lives. On August 8, during their first visit to the Hernandez home, the group noted a foul odor in the house, heard noises in the attic, and captured glowing orbs of light in photographs. Skeptical of Jackie's claim of seeing a phantom head in the attic, Wheatcraft took several photos in the darkened space. But he left the room in terror after an unseen force yanked the camera from his hands. When he summoned the courage to go back into the attic (this time with a flashlight), he found the body of the camera on one side of the room and the lens on the other, inside a box.

Later that same evening, while Wheatcraft and Conrad were in the attic, Wheatcraft was violently pushed by an invisible hand. After they returned to the main level of the house, loud banging noises were heard coming from the attic, as if someone (or something) was stomping above them.

When the researchers returned to the house later that month, they observed a liquid oozing from the walls and dripping from the cabinets. Samples that were analyzed at a lab determined that the substance was blood plasma from a human male.

Why it would be oozing from the walls was anyone's guess.

GET OUT AND DON'T LOOK BACK

The phenomena that Jackie and the investigators experienced on the night of September 4, 1989, shook them to their very cores. During the day, the poltergeist ramped up its attention-seeking behavior. After watching objects fly through the air and hearing mysterious moaning and breathing noises, Jackie called the researchers for help.

Wheatcraft and Conrad's friend Gary Boehm were inspecting the pitch-black attic and were just about to leave when Wheatcraft screamed. Boehm took a photo hoping that the flash would illuminate the room so he could see Wheatcraft and help him. Boehm's photo captured the spirit's latest attack on Wheatcraft, who was hanging from the rafters with a clothesline wrapped around his neck; the cord was tied with a seaman's knot. Boehm was able to rescue Wheatcraft, who was understandably shaken by his encounter with the evil entity that seemed to have a personal vendetta against him.

After observing several other paranormal phenomena that night, Jackie and the researchers left the San Pedro house, never to return.

YOU CAN RUN BUT YOU CAN'T HIDE

Frightened for the safety of her young children, Jackie moved her family nearly 200 miles away to

Weldon, California. But it didn't take long for the poltergeist to find her. The haunting started with unusual scratching noises that came from a backyard shed; then, a black, shapeless form was spotted in the hallway of the home. As had been the case in San Pedro, others witnessed the phenomena as well: While moving an old television set out of the storage shed, Jackie's neighbors saw the ghostly image of an old man on the screen.

In April 1990, when the researchers heard that the paranormal activity had followed Jackie to her new home, they drove to Weldon to continue their work on the case. Besides, Wheatcraft had a personal interest in the matter: He wanted to know why the entity was focusing its physical attacks on him.

Hoping to provoke the spirit, Jackie, her friend, and the researchers decided to use a Ouija board. During the session, the table that they used shook violently, candles flickered, and the temperature in the room dropped dramatically. But the group may have received the answers it was seeking: Through the Ouija board, the spirit told them that he was a sailor who had been murdered in 1930 when his killer drowned him in San Pedro Bay. He also said that his killer had lived in Jackie's former home in San Pedro.

When Wheatcraft asked the spirit why he was being targeted, the entity said that Wheatcraft resembled his killer. It then picked up Wheatcraft and threw him against the wall. He was naturally frightened, but he was not injured.

After that, Conrad searched old newspaper records to see if the information that they'd received from the spirit could be verified; it was. In 1930, sailor Herman Hendrickson was found drowned in San Pedro Bay. Although he'd also suffered a fractured skull, his death was ruled accidental. Perhaps Hendrickson's spirit was attemping to make it known that his death was not accidental but that he was murdered.

SPIRIT STALKER

In June 1990, Jackie moved back to San Pedro and rented an apartment on Seventh Street. This time, she had a priest bless the place before she moved in. Nevertheless, the glowing orbs of light returned.

Later that year, Conrad's home was also infested with poltergeist activity, which he witnessed along with Boehm and Wheatcraft. Objects were mysteriously moved to new locations, burners on the gas stove turned on by themselves, scissors flew across the kitchen, a broom was left standing on top of the stove, and scissors were found underneath pillows in the bedroom. Also, Wheatcraft was again pushed by the invisible force, which left red scratch marks on his back.

The phenomena greatly diminished after that, although subsequent residents of the house on 11th Street in San Pedro also claimed to witness poltergeist activity; since then, it is said that no one has lived in the house for more than six months.

Although Jackie was terribly frightened by the mysterious activity at the time, she later said that she was grateful to have had a firsthand encounter with the Other Side, which not many people get to experience. Although some folks might welcome a visit from a ghost, few would want it to be as distressing as what Jackie went through.

GHOSTS LIVE ON AT THE CLOVIS SANITARIUM

Picture this scene at the emergency call center in Clovis, California: "Hello. 911. What's your emergency?" Dead silence. "Hello? Is anyone there?" More silence. So the dispatcher checks to see where the call is coming from and finds that it's 2604 Clovis Avenue: the former home of the Clovis Sanitarium—a building that has no electricity and no working phone. It's probably not a life-or-death situation, since whatever is making the call is already dead.

THE HISTORY

Oddly, this type of phone call is not uncommon in Clovis—a city of 95,000 that is located just northeast of Fresno. Nicknamed "the Gateway to the Sierras," Clovis was the home of Anthony Andriotti, who built a magnificent mansion for his family in 1922.

Unfortunately, he miscalculated the cost of the building's upkeep, and he went bankrupt, turned to alcohol and opium, and died in 1929 at age 36.

The estate sat empty until it was reopened in 1935 as the Hazelwood Sanitarium for tuberculosis patients. In 1942, it became the Clovis Avenue Sanitarium, which was dedicated to serving the area's physically and mentally ill.

A PLACE TO DIE

Families whose loved ones suffered from dementia or schizophrenia brought these unfortunate souls to the Clovis Sanitarium to die. It is said that at one point, the death rate at the facility reached an average of one person per day. Still, the building soon became overcrowded, with ten beds to a room and one nurse overseeing two or more rooms. Former employees told sad tales of patients who were abused and neglected.

When patients died, their bodies were stored in the relatively cool basement until they could be removed. Locals started talking about strange happenings at the sanitarium, and rumors began to suggest that the place was haunted. But it wasn't all idle gossip: It seems that there *were* some pretty strange things going on at 2604 Clovis Avenue.

A CALL FOR HELP

In 1992, the Clovis Sanitarium closed; that's when the mysterious phone calls began. Sometimes neighbors or passersby would call the police regarding trespassers or vandals. But then there were the other calls—the ones that came directly from the vacant building that had no working phone line.

Unfazed by these odd stories, Todd Wolfe bought the property in 1997 with hopes of creating a haunted-house-type Halloween attraction. Initially a skeptic, Wolfe was surprised when his employees complained about spirits interfering with their work. They saw apparitions and reported being touched and grabbed by unseen hands. It wasn't until he had his own encounter in "Mary's Room"—where he actually saw a shadowy apparition—that Wolfe began to believe. Today, Mary's Room is furnished with only original furniture because it seems that "Mary" gets quite upset when changes are made. And a disturbed Mary leads to increased paranormal activity, including phantom breathing, shoving by an invisible force, and objects that move seemingly on their own.

Many paranormal groups have visited the Clovis Sanitarium, and all agree that it is indeed haunted. They've heard shuffling footsteps and strange voices, and many have reported feelings of being watched.

ENERGETIC SPIRITS

When the *Ghost Adventures* team visited the Clovis Sanitarium in a 2010 episode, they were greeted by a laughing spirit and a spike in electromagnetic energy (in a building with no electricity). Later, in the basement, the crew used a state-of-the-art ultraviolet camera to record a mysterious purple form; the shape even appeared to sit on a couch for a while. The team also captured some amazing

EVPs (electronic voice phenomena), including one that told the group to "Get out" and another that said it wanted their energy.

Investigator Zak Bagans observed that the ghosts of Clovis Sanitarium are an unusual bunch. The original owners were a family with young children who lived a lavish lifestyle, full of happiness and laughter. But combine those feelings with those of the mentally ill who were neglected and abused after being brought there to die, and the mix becomes volatile. As Bagans concluded, "That contrasting energy has to do something weird to the atmosphere."

SAN DIEGO GHOSTS GATHER AT THE WHALEY HOUSE

Even if you don't believe in ghosts, you've got to be intrigued by all the chatter surrounding the Whaley House in San Diego. According to late ghost hunter Hans Holzer, this old family homestead might be the most haunted house in America. The U.S. Department of Commerce lists the building as an authentic Haunted House (it is one of only two structures in the country—along with the Winchester Mystery House—to hold this distinction), and the television show America's Most Haunted *called it the Most Haunted House in the United States.*

HOW IT ALL BEGAN

The first two-story building in San Diego and now the oldest on the West Coast, the Whaley House needs all of its space to house the many spirits that reside inside it.

Built by prominent Californian Thomas Whaley in 1856, it began as a one-story granary with an adjacent two-story residence. By the next year, Whaley had opened a general store on the premises. Over the years, the building also served as a county courthouse, a ballroom, a billiards hall, and a theater, among other things. Now it's a California State Historic Landmark and a museum.

SQUATTER'S RIGHTS

Hindsight is always $^{20}/_{20}$, but perhaps Thomas Whaley should have thought twice about buying the property on which "Yankee Jim" Robinson was publicly hanged in 1852. Accused of attempted grand larceny, Robinson was executed in a particularly unpleasant display. The gallows were situated on the back of a wagon that was set up at the site; however, being a tall man, Yankee Jim was able to reach the wagon with his feet, thus delaying his death for several minutes. According to newspaper reports, when his legs were finally pulled out from under him, he "swung back and forth like a pendulum" until he died. Not a pretty sight.

Although Whaley was actually present at Robinson's execution, he apparently didn't associate the property with the gruesome event that had taken place there. Nevertheless, soon after the house was completed, he and his family began to hear heavy disembodied footsteps, as if a large man was walking through the house. Remembering what had taken place there a few years earlier, the Whaleys believed that the spirit of Yankee Jim himself was sharing their new home. Apparently, Robinson was not a malevolent ghost because the Whaleys' youngest daughter,

Lillian, remained in the house with the spirit until 1953. But to this day, visitors to the site still report hearing the heavy-footed phantom.

FAMILY SPIRITS

After the house became a historic landmark and was opened to the public in 1960, staff, tourists, and ghost hunters alike began to experience paranormal phenomena such as apparitions, noises, and isolated cold spots. Some have even caught glimpses of a small spotted dog running by with its ears flapping, which just might be the spirit of the Whaleys' terrier, Dolly Varden.

Although Thomas and Anna Whaley lived in several different houses, the couple must have dearly loved their original San Diego home because they don't seem quite ready to leave it, even a century after their deaths. They have been seen—and heard—going about their daily business and doing chores in the house. Don't they know there's a cleaning service for that?

The couple has also been captured on film acting as though it was still the 19th century. Thomas was seen wandering through the house and smoking a pipe near an upstairs window, while Anna seems to have kept up her duties as the matron of the house: People have seen her rocking a baby, tucking a child into bed, and folding clothes. Sometimes, the family's rocking chair is seen teetering back and forth all by itself. Children are especially likely to see the building's former occupants. Employees frequently notice youngsters smiling or waving at people who the adults are unable to see. And the sound of piano music that sometimes drifts through the air? Most say that it's Anna, still playing the tunes that she loved most in life.

Long before he became one of America's most beloved TV personalities, Regis Philbin worked at a television station in San Diego. In 1964, when he and a companion paid a visit to the Whaley House to investigate the ghostly tales, Philbin was startled to see the wispy figure of Anna Whaley moving along one of the walls. When he turned on a flashlight to get a better look, she disappeared, leaving only her portrait to smile back at him.

WILTED VIOLET

Thomas and Anna's daughter Violet had a particularly sad life and is thought to haunt the old house where she once lived. In 1882, in a double wedding with her sister Anna Amelia, the beautiful Violet was married at the Whaley House to a man that her parents did not trust. Unfortunately, the marriage lasted only two weeks, after which Violet was granted a divorce. Divorce was highly uncommon in those days, and the scandal was humiliating for both Violet and her family. Violet became extremely depressed, and in 1885, she took her own life by shooting herself in the heart.

It is believed that Violet makes her presence known by turning on lights in the upstairs rooms and setting off the burglar alarm. Her spirit is also thought to be responsible for the phantom footsteps that emanate from the second floor and the sudden icy chills often felt by visitors—as though a spirit had just walked right through them.

GHOSTS GALORE

Most of the spirits at the Whaley House seem to be related to the family or the site. A young girl has been seen in several locations in and around the house. Dressed in 19th-century clothing, she plays with toys in the playroom, sniffs flowers in the garden, and darts in and out of the dining room very quickly. Some say that she was a playmate of the Whaley children and that she died on the property when she got tangled in a clothesline and either broke her neck or was strangled; however, there is no record of such a death occurring at the Whaley House. Others say that although her spirit is real, her story was made up somewhere along the way, which only adds to the intrigue of the place. As if there wasn't enough of that already.

Another female ghost seems to be attached to the part of the house that once served as a courtroom. One visitor said that as she walked into the room, she saw a woman dressed in a calico skirt typical of the 1800s. The spirit didn't seem evil, but it didn't seem to be particularly welcoming either. The visitor captured the spectral woman's shadowy figure in a photo. It seems likely that the ghost is somehow connected to an event that took place in the courtroom.

The ghost of a man dressed in a businesslike frock coat has also appeared in the former courtroom. However, his spirit may not be strongly attached to the building because it fades away more quickly than others that are seen there.

HAUNTED HAPPENINGS

In addition to these apparitions, visitors, volunteers, and employees have reported other odd phenomena inside the house. Unexplained singing, organ music, and whistling have been heard, as has a toddler crying in an upstairs nursery. (This is believed to be the spirit of Thomas and Anna's son, who was also named Thomas; he died of scarlet fever at age 17 months.) Some have witnessed levitating furniture, and others have noticed mysterious scents, such as perfume, cigar smoke, and the scent of holiday baking coming from an empty kitchen.

When visitors first enter the house, they can examine photos taken by previous visitors. These images all have one thing in common: They contain mysterious objects such as shadows, orbs, and misty figures. One visitor reported trying to take photos with an otherwise reliable camera; as soon as she tried to focus, the camera beeped, indicating that she was too close to her subject despite the fact that she was nowhere near the closest (visible) object. Once developed, the photos featured an orb or filmy shadow in nearly every shot.

At least the Whaley House spirits take some responsibility for the place. Once, after an especially long day at the museum, a staff member was getting ready to close up when all the doors and windows on both floors suddenly locked on their own, all at the same time. Sometimes spirits just need a little alone time.

WINCHESTER MYSTERY HOUSE

By the time she was 22, Sarah Pardee was seriously popular—she spoke four languages, played the piano, and was exceedingly pretty. Nicknamed the "Belle of New Haven," she had her pick of suitors.

She chose a young man named William W. Winchester, the only son of Oliver Winchester, a stockholder with the successful New Haven Arms Company. When Sarah and William married in 1862, William had plans to expand the business by buying out some of his competition and introducing the repeating rifle, so named because its lever action allowed a gunman to fire many shots in succession. The gun became known as "The Gun that Won the West," and the now fabulously wealthy Winchester name was woven into the fabric of American history.

CAN'T BUY ME LOVE

In the summer of 1866, Sarah gave birth to a daughter, but the joy of a new baby was brief. The child was born sickly, diagnosed with marasmus, a protein deficiency that typically afflicts infants in third-world countries. The baby was unable to gain weight and succumbed to the disease in just a few weeks.

Sarah and William were both bereft, but Sarah took it the hardest. She sank into a serious depression from which she would never totally recover.

Fifteen years later, when Oliver Winchester passed away, William stepped into his dad's shoes at the family business.

However, he had only held the job for a few months when he lost a battle with tuberculosis and died in 1881.

Sarah was now 41 years old and without the family she had built her life around. She was also extremely wealthy. In the late 1880s, the average family income hovered around $500 per year. Sarah was pulling in about $1,000 per day! Because her husband left her everything, she had more than 700 shares of stock in addition to income from current sales. Sarah was up to her eyeballs in money. When William's mother died in 1898, Sarah inherited 2,000 more shares, which meant that she owned about 50 percent of the business. Sarah Winchester was all dressed up and had absolutely nowhere to go—even if she did have someplace, there was no one with whom she could share it.

"I SEE DEAD PEOPLE"

Today, most people regard psychics with more than a little suspicion and skepticism, but in the late 19th century, psychics had grabbed much of the public's attention and trust. The period after the Civil War and the onslaught of new industry had left so much destruction and created so much change for people that many were looking for answers in a confusing world. With claims that they could commune with the "Great Beyond," psychics were consulted by thousands hoping for some insight.

Sarah was not doing well after the death of her husband. Losing her child had been a debilitating blow, but after her husband's passing, she was barely able to function. Fearing for her life, one of Sarah's close friends suggested she visit a psychic to see if she could contact her husband or daughter or both.

Sarah agreed to visit a Boston medium named Adam Coons, who wasted no time in telling her that William was trying to communicate with her, and the message wasn't good.

Apparently, William was desperate to tell Sarah that the family was cursed as a result of the invention of the repeating rifle. Native Americans, settlers, and soldiers all over the world were dead, largely due to the Winchester family. The spirits of these people were out for Sarah next, said William through the medium. The only way for her to prolong her life was to "head toward the setting sun," which meant, "move to California." The medium told her that once she got there, she would have to build a house where all those spirits could live happily together—but the house had to be built big and built often. Sarah was told that construction on the house could never cease, or the spirits would claim her and she would die. So Sarah packed up and left New Haven for California in 1884.

NOW THAT'S A HOUSE!

Sarah bought an eight-room farmhouse on the outskirts of the burgeoning town of San Jose, on the southern end of San Francisco Bay. Legend has it that she hired more than 20 workmen and a foreman and kept them working 24 hours a day, 365 days a year. To ensure that they would keep quiet about what they were doing—and not leave because the house was more than a little weird—

she paid them a whopping $3 per day—more than twice the going rate of the time.

The workmen took the money and built as their client wished, though it made no sense whatsoever. Sarah was not an architect, but she gave the orders for the house's design. Sarah's odd requests, the constant construction, and an endless stream of money resulted in a rather unusual abode—stairs lead to ceilings, windows open into brick walls, and some rooms have no doors. There are also Tiffany windows all over the place, many containing the number 13, with which Sarah was obsessed. There are spiderweb-paned windows, which, although lovely, didn't do much to dispel rumors that Sarah was preoccupied with death and the occult.

The house kept on growing, all because the spirits were supposedly "advising" Sarah. Chimneys were built and never used. There were so many rooms that counting them was pointless. Reportedly, one stairway in the house went up seven steps and down eleven, and one of the linen closets is bigger than most three-bedroom apartments.

Very few people ever saw the lady of the house. When she shopped in town, merchants came to her car, as she rarely stepped out.
Rumors were rampant in San Jose: Who was this crazy lady? Was the house haunted by spirits or just the energy of the aggrieved widow who

lived there? Would the hammers ever stop banging? The workers knew how weird the house was, but no one knew for sure what went on inside Sarah's head.

Still, Sarah was generous in the community. She donated to the poor, occasionally socialized, and, in the early days, even threw a party every once in a while. She had a maid she was quite fond of and was exceedingly kind to any children she encountered. But as the house grew and the years passed, the rumors became more prevalent and the increasingly private Winchester retreated further into her bizarre hermitage.

THE END

In 1922, Sarah Winchester died in her sleep, and the construction finally ceased after 38 years. In her will, Sarah left huge chunks of her estate to nieces, nephews, and loyal employees. The will was divided into exactly 13 parts and was signed 13 times. Her belongings, everything from ornate furniture to chandeliers to silver dinner services, were auctioned off. It took six weeks to remove everything.

And as for the house itself, it wasn't going to find a buyer any time soon: The structure at the time of Sarah's passing covered several acres and had more than 10,000 window panes, 160 rooms, 467 doorways, 47 fireplaces, 40 stairways, and 6 kitchens. A group of investors bought the house in hopes of turning it into a tourist attraction, which they did. What they didn't do was employ guides or security, however, so for a small fee, thousands of curious people came from all over the country to traipse through the house, scribbling graffiti on the walls and stealing bits of wallpaper. It wasn't until the house was purchased in the 1970s and renamed the Winchester Mystery House that it was restored to its original state. Millions of people have visited the house, which continues to be one of the top tourist attractions in California.

THE FOOTNOTE

With so many people going in and out of the house over the years, it's not surprising that there are tales of "strange happenings" in the Winchester mansion. People have claimed that they've heard and seen banging doors, mysterious voices, cold spots, moving lights, doorknobs that turn by themselves, and more than a few say that Sarah herself still roams the many rooms. Psychics who have visited the house solemnly swear that it is indeed haunted.

THE GHOSTS OF YOSEMITE NATIONAL PARK

Anyone with an ounce of supernatural savvy knows that anything connected with Native American burial grounds and/or curses is like a flashing yellow caution light saying, "Warning: Paranormal Activity Ahead."

THE CREEPY CANYON

Back in the 19th century, the ability of Native Americans to marshal the wrath of the spirit world was dismissed as superstitious mumbo-jumbo. That's unfortunate, because if it had been taken more seriously, people might have feared the consequences of the words of Chief Tenaya of the

Ahwahneechee tribe. In 1851, when white settlers were trying to force his people out of the Yosemite Valley in what is now Yosemite National Park, Chief Tenaya put a curse on the land.

It turns out that the chief wasn't just making an idle gesture. In the park's Tenaya Canyon, a disproportionate number of tragic incidents have occurred: Visitors to the area have become lost, drowned, fallen to their deaths, and died of hypothermia. Once, a pilot who was looking for an injured hiker was purportedly overcome by vertigo and nearly flew his chopper into the side of the canyon. Not even Yosemite champion John Muir was spared from the alleged curse: During his first visit to the canyon, Muir fell and was knocked unconscious while scaling cliffs in "the Bermuda Triangle of Yosemite," as Tenaya Canyon is sometimes called.

Apparently, Tenaya is not above more forceful demonstrations to exact his revenge. In 1996, a Native American who had been born in the park and had spent his entire life working there as a maintenance technician was preparing to retire. At that time, park officials were told that Ahwahneechee legend warned that the last Yosemite-born Indian's departure from the park would bring disaster. But in late December 1996, with their heads firmly buried in the sand, park officials let the man retire and leave the confines of the park.

A few days later, on January 1, a freak storm resulted in a flood that caused $178 million in damage to the park. Some months later (and possibly with a nervous nod to

Tenaya), park officials agreed to establish a traditional Native American village in Yosemite Valley.

Sometimes Tenaya steps aside and allows others to do the supernatural heavy lifting at Yosemite. Visitors to the park have reported seeing and even speaking with Native American apparitions. Legends tell of a ghost boy that inhabits the waters of Grouse Lake; he reportedly likes to grab the legs of swimmers and pull them underneath the water. It is also said that an evil spirit wind inhabits Bridalveil Fall and that this wind is always ready to send an unsuspecting soul plummeting into the falls to his or her death.

A GHOSTLY GROUP

Some standard hauntings round out the supernatural smorgasbord at Yosemite. According to legend, a lonely camper once hung himself in his tent; late at night, his body can supposedly still be seen slowly swinging forlornly from the tent frame. Also, a young couple who drowned near Stoneman Bridge has been seen on or near the span on many occasions.

Yosemite's Ahwahnee Hotel is the park's own "Apparition Inn." The building was used as a convalescent home for soldiers during World War II, and it is believed that many of its ghosts are the spirits of those troops. The hotel's former operator, Mary Curry Tresidder, lived in the building for many years until she died in the 1960s, and apparently, she isn't letting a little thing like death force her to check out: She's still seen on the sixth floor, perhaps making certain that the guests are comfortable.

However, for sheer spiritual star power, nothing can top the phantom rocking chair that appears from time to time on the third floor. In 1962, President John F. Kennedy stayed in a third-floor suite, and the hotel placed a rocking chair in the room for his comfort. The chair was removed after Kennedy left; however, since his assassination in 1963, housekeepers have witnessed a rocking chair slowly swaying back and forth in the room in which he stayed. When they glance away from the chair, it disappears.

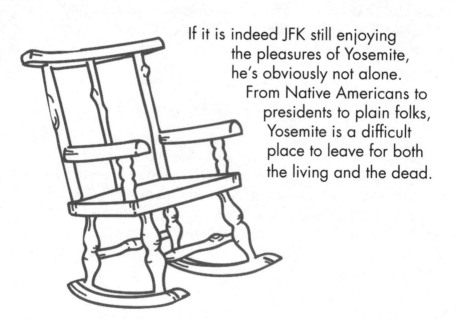

If it is indeed JFK still enjoying the pleasures of Yosemite, he's obviously not alone. From Native Americans to presidents to plain folks, Yosemite is a difficult place to leave for both the living and the dead.